Django Girls Tutorial

A catalogue record for this book is available from the Hong Kong Public Libraries.

Published in Hong Kong by Samurai Media Limited.

Email: info@samuraimedia.org

ISBN 978-988-8407-20-0

Table of Contents

Django Girls Tutorial

Welcome

Welcome to the Django Girls Tutorial! We are happy to see you here :) In this tutorial, we will take you on a journey under the hood of web technologies, offering you a glimpse of all the bits and pieces that need to come together to make the web work as we know it.

As with all unknown things, this is going to be an adventure - but no worries, since you already worked up the courage to be here, you'll be just fine :)

Introduction

Have you ever felt that the world is more and more about technology to which you cannot (yet) relate? Have you ever wondered how to create a website but have never had enough motivation to start? Have you ever thought that the software world is too complicated for you to even try doing something on your own?

Well, we have good news for you! Programming is not as hard as it seems and we want to show you how fun it can be.

This tutorial will not magically turn you into a programmer. If you want to be good at it, you need months or even years of learning and practice. But we want to show you that programming or creating websites is not as complicated as it seems. We will try to explain different bits and pieces as well as we can, so you will not feel intimidated by technology.

We hope that we'll be able to make you love technology as much as we do!

What will you learn during the tutorial?

Once you've finished the tutorial, you will have a simple, working web application: your own blog. We will show you how to put it online, so others will see your work!

It will (more or less) look like this:

If you work with the tutorial on your own and don't have a coach who will help you in case of any problem, we have a chat system for you: **chat on gitter**. We asked our coaches and previous attendees to be there from time to time and help others with the tutorial! Don't be afraid to ask your question there!

OK, let's start at the beginning...

Following the tutorial at home

It is amazing to take part in a Django Girls workshop, but we are aware that it is not always possible to attend one. This is why we encourage you to try following this tutorial at home. For readers at home we are currently preparing videos that will make it easier to follow the tutorial on your own. It is still a work in progress, but more and more things will be covered soon at the Coding is for girls YouTube channel.

In every chapter already covered, there is a link that points to the correct video.

About and contributing

This tutorial is maintained by DjangoGirls. If you find any mistakes or want to update the tutorial please follow the contributing guidelines.

Would you like to help us translate the tutorial to other languages?

Currently, translations are being kept on crowdin.com platform at:

https://crowdin.com/project/django-girls-tutorial

If your language is not listed on crowdin, please open a new issue informing us of the language so we can add it.

If you're doing the tutorial at home

If you're doing the tutorial at home, not at one of the Django Girls events, you can completely skip this chapter now and go straight to the How the Internet works chapter.

This is because we cover these things in the whole tutorial anyway, and this is just an additional page that gathers all of the installation instructions in one place. The Django Girls event includes one "Installation evening" where we install everything so we don't need to bother with it during the workshop, so this is useful for us.

If you find it useful, you can follow through this chapter too. But if you want to start learning things before installing a bunch of stuff on your computer, skip this chapter and we will explain the installation part to you later on.

Good luck!

Installation

In the workshop you will be building a blog, and there are a few setup tasks in the tutorial which would be good to work through beforehand so that you are ready to start coding on the day.

Chromebook setup (if you're using one)

You can skip right over this section if you're not using a Chromebook. If you are, your installation experience will be a little different. You can ignore the rest of the installation instructions.

Cloud 9

Cloud 9 is a tool that gives you a code editor and access to a computer running on the Internet where you can install, write, and run software. For the duration of the tutorial, Cloud 9 will act as your *local machine*. You'll still be running commands in a terminal interface just like your classmates on OS X, Ubuntu, or Windows, but your terminal will be connected to a computer running somewhere else that Cloud 9 sets up for you.

1. Install Cloud 9 from the Chrome web store
2. Go to c9.io
3. Sign up for an account
4. Click *Create a New Workspace*
5. Name it *django-girls*
6. Select the *Blank* (second from the right on the bottom row with orange logo)

Now you should see an interface with a sidebar, a big main window with some text, and a small window at the bottom that looks something like this:

Cloud 9

```
yourusername:~/workspace $
```

This bottom area is your *terminal*, where you will give the computer Cloud 9 has prepared for you instructions. You can resize that window to make it a bit bigger.

Virtual Environment

A virtual environment (also called a virtualenv) is like a private box we can stuff useful computer code into for a project we're working on. We use them to keep the various bits of code we want for our various projects separate so things don't get mixed up between projects.

In your terminal at the bottom of the Cloud 9 interface, run the following:

Cloud 9

```
sudo apt install python3.5-venv
```

If this still doesn't work, ask your coach for some help.

Next, run:

Cloud 9

```
mkdir djangogirls
cd djangogirls
python3.5 -mvenv myvenv
source myvenv/bin/activate
pip install django~=1.10.0
```

(note that on the last line we use a tilde followed by an equal sign: ~=).

Github

Make a Github account.

PythonAnywhere

The Django Girls tutorial includes a section on what is called Deployment, which is the process of taking the code that powers your new web application and moving it to a publicly accessible computer (called a server) so other people can see your work.

This part is a little odd when doing the tutorial on a Chromebook since we're already using a computer that is on the Internet (as opposed to, say, a laptop). However, it's still useful, as we can think of our Cloud 9 workspace as a place or our "in progress" work and Python Anywhere as a place to show off our stuff as it becomes more complete.

Thus, sign up for a new Python Anywhere account at www.pythonanywhere.com.

Install Python

> For readers at home: this chapter is covered in the Installing Python & Code Editor video.

> This section is based on a tutorial by Geek Girls Carrots (https://github.com/ggcarrots/django-carrots)

Django is written in Python. We need Python to do anything in Django. Let's start by installing it! We want you to install Python 3.5, so if you have any earlier version, you will need to upgrade it.

Windows

First check whether your computer is running a 32-bit version or a 64-bit version of Windows at https://support.microsoft.com/en-au/kb/827218. You can download Python for Windows from the website https://www.python.org/downloads/windows/. Click on the "Latest Python 3 Release - Python x.x.x" link. If your computer is running a **64-bit** version of Windows, download the **Windows x86-64 executable installer**. Otherwise, download the **Windows x86 executable installer**. After downloading the installer, you should run it (double-click on it) and follow the instructions there.

One thing to watch out for: During the installation you will notice a window marked "Setup". Make sure you tick the "Add Python 3.5 to PATH" checkbox and click on "Install Now", as shown here:

In upcoming steps, you'll be using the Windows Command Line (which we'll also tell you about). For now, if you need to type in some commands, go to Start menu → All Programs → Accessories → Command Prompt. You can also hold in the Windows key and press the "R"-key until the "Run" window pops up. To open the Command Line, type "cmd" and press enter in the "Run" window. (On newer versions of Windows, you might have to search for "Command Prompt" since it's sometimes hidden.)

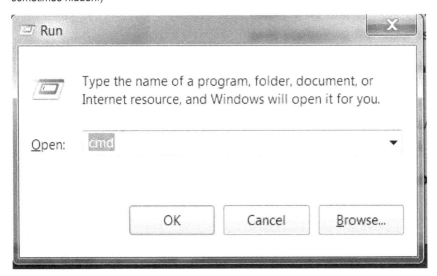

Note: if you are using an older version of Windows (7, Vista, or any older version) and the Python 3.5.x installer fails with an error, you can try either:

1. install all Windows Updates and try to install Python 3.5 again; or
2. install an older version of Python, e.g., 3.4.4.

If you install an older version of Python, the installation screen may look a bit different than shown above. Make sure you scroll down to see "Add python.exe to Path", then click the button on the left and pick "Will be installed on local hard drive":

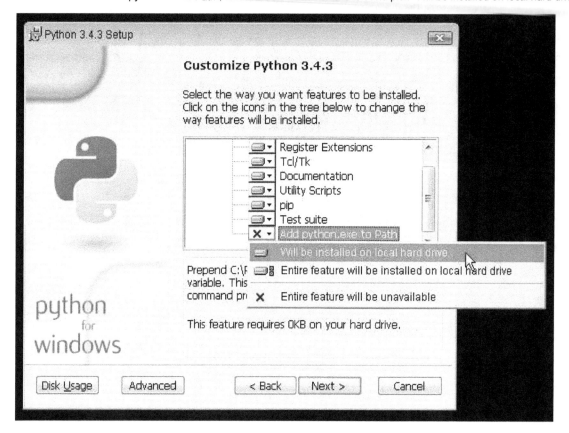

OS X

You need to go to the website https://www.python.org/downloads/release/python-351/ and download the Python installer:

- Download the *Mac OS X 64-bit/32-bit installer* file,
- Double click *python-3.5.1-macosx10.6.pkg* to run the installer.

Linux

It is very likely that you already have Python installed out of the box. To check if you have it installed (and which version it is), open a console and type the following command:

command-line

```
$ python3 --version
Python 3.5.1
```

If you have a different 'micro version' of Python installed, e.g. 3.5.0, then you don't have to upgrade. If you don't have Python installed, or if you want a different version, you can install it as follows:

Debian or Ubuntu

Type this command into your console:

command-line

```
$ sudo apt-get install python3.5
```

Fedora (up to 21)

Use this command in your console:

command-line

```
$ sudo yum install python3
```

Fedora (22+)

Use this command in your console:

command-line

```
$ sudo dnf install python3
```

openSUSE

Use this command in your console:

command-line

```
$ sudo zypper install python3
```

Verify the installation was successful by opening the *Terminal* application and running the `python3` command:

command-line

```
$ python3 --version
Python 3.5.1
```

NOTE: If you're on Windows and you get an error message that `python3` wasn't found, try using `python` (without the `3`) and check if it still might be a version of Python 3.5.

If you have any doubts, or if something went wrong and you have no idea what to do next, please ask your coach! Sometimes things don't go smoothly and it's better to ask for help from someone with more experience.

Set up virtualenv and install Django

Part of this section is based on tutorials by Geek Girls Carrots (https://github.com/ggcarrots/django-carrots).

Part of this section is based on the django-marcador tutorial licensed under the Creative Commons Attribution-ShareAlike 4.0 International License. The django-marcador tutorial is copyrighted by Markus Zapke-Gründemann et al.

Virtual environment

Before we install Django we will get you to install an extremely useful tool to help keep your coding environment tidy on your computer. It's possible to skip this step, but it's highly recommended. Starting with the best possible setup will save you a lot of trouble in the future!

So, let's create a **virtual environment** (also called a *virtualenv*). Virtualenv will isolate your Python/Django setup on a per-project basis. This means that any changes you make to one website won't affect any others you're also developing. Neat, right?

All you need to do is find a directory in which you want to create the `virtualenv` ; your home directory, for example. On Windows it might look like `C:\Users\Name\` (where `Name` is the name of your login).

NOTE: On Windows, make sure that this directory does not contain accented or special characters; if your username contains accented characters, use a different directory, for example `c:\djangogirls` .

For this tutorial we will be using a new directory `djangogirls` from your home directory:

command-line

```
$ mkdir djangogirls
$ cd djangogirls
```

We will make a virtualenv called `myvenv` . The general command will be in the format:

command-line

```
$ python3 -m venv myvenv
```

Windows

To create a new `virtualenv` , you need to open the console (we told you about that a few chapters ago – remember?) and run `C:\Python35\python -m venv myvenv` . It will look like this:

command-line

```
C:\Users\Name\djangogirls> C:\Python35\python -m venv myvenv
```

where `C:\Python35\python` is the directory in which you previously installed Python and `myvenv` is the name of your `virtualenv` . You can use any other name, but stick to lowercase and use no spaces, accents or special characters. It is also good idea to keep the name short – you'll be referencing it a lot!

Linux and OS X

Creating a `virtualenv` on both Linux and OS X is as simple as running `python3 -m venv myvenv` . It will look like this:

command-line

```
$ python3 -m venv myvenv
```

`myvenv` is the name of your `virtualenv`. You can use any other name, but stick to lowercase and use no spaces. It is also good idea to keep the name short as you'll be referencing it a lot!

NOTE: On some versions of Debian/Ubuntu you may receive the following error:

command-line

```
The virtual environment was not created successfully because ensurepip is not available.  On Debian/Ubuntu sys
tems, you need to install the python3-venv package using the following command.
    apt-get install python3-venv
You may need to use sudo with that command.  After installing the python3-venv package, recreate your virtual
environment.
```

In this case, follow the instructions above and install the `python3-venv` package:

command-line

```
$ sudo apt-get install python3-venv
```

NOTE: On some versions of Debian/Ubuntu initiating the virtual environment like this currently gives the following error:

command-line

```
Error: Command '['/home/eddie/Slask/tmp/venv/bin/python3', '-Im', 'ensurepip', '--upgrade', '--default-pip']'
returned non-zero exit status 1
```

To get around this, use the `virtualenv` command instead.

command-line

```
$ sudo apt-get install python-virtualenv
$ virtualenv --python=python3.5 myvenv
```

NOTE: If you get an error like

command-line

```
E: Unable to locate package python3-venv
```

then instead run:

command-line

```
sudo apt install python3.5-venv
```

Working with virtualenv

The command above will create a directory called `myvenv` (or whatever name you chose) that contains our virtual environment (basically a bunch of directory and files).

Windows

Start your virtual environment by running:

command-line

```
C:\Users\Name\djangogirls> myvenv\Scripts\activate
```

NOTE: on Windows 10 you might get an error in the Windows PowerShell that says execution of scripts is disabled on this system . In this case, open another Windows PowerShell with the "Run as Administrator" option. Then try typing the following command before starting your virtual environment:

command-line

```
C:\WINDOWS\system32> Set-ExecutionPolicy -ExecutionPolicy RemoteSigned
    Execution Policy Change
    The execution policy helps protect you from scripts that you do not trust. Changing the execution policy m
ight expose you to the security risks described in the about_Execution_Policies help topic at http://go.micros
oft.com/fwlink/?LinkID=135170. Do you want to change the execution policy? [Y] Yes  [A] Yes to All  [N] No  [L
] No to All  [S] Suspend  [?] Help (default is "N"): A
```

Linux and OS X

Start your virtual environment by running:

command-line

```
$ source myvenv/bin/activate
```

Remember to replace myvenv with your chosen virtualenv name!

NOTE: sometimes source might not be available. In those cases try doing this instead:

command-line

```
$ . myvenv/bin/activate
```

You will know that you have virtualenv started when you see that the prompt in your console is prefixed with (myvenv) .

When working within a virtual environment, python will automatically refer to the correct version so you can use python instead of python3 .

OK, we have all important dependencies in place. We can finally install Django!

Installing Django

Now that you have your virtualenv started, you can install Django.

Before we do that, we should make sure we have the latest version of pip , the software that we use to install Django:

command-line

```
(myvenv) ~$ pip install --upgrade pip
```

Then run pip install django~=1.10.0 (note that we use a tilde followed by an equal sign: ~=) to install Django.

command-line

```
(myvenv) ~$ pip install django~=1.10.0
Collecting django~=1.10.0
  Downloading Django-1.10.4-py2.py3-none-any.whl (6.8MB)
Installing collected packages: django
Successfully installed django-1.10.4
```

Windows

If you get an error when calling pip on Windows platform, please check if your project pathname contains spaces, accents or special characters (for example, `C:\Users\User Name\djangogirls`). If it does, please consider using another place without spaces, accents or special characters (suggestion: `C:\djangogirls`). Create a new virtualenv in the new directory, then delete the old one and try the above command again. (Moving the virtualenv directory won't work since virtualenv uses absolute paths.)

Windows 8 and Windows 10

Your command line might freeze after when you try to install Django. If this happens, instead of the above command use:

command-line

```
C:\Users\Name\djangogirls> python -m pip install django~=1.10.0
```

Linux

If you get an error when calling pip on Ubuntu 12.04 please run `python -m pip install -U --force-reinstall pip` to fix the pip installation in the virtualenv.

That's it! You're now (finally) ready to create a Django application!

Install a code editor

There are a lot of different editors and it largely boils down to personal preference. Most Python programmers use complex but extremely powerful IDEs (Integrated Development Environments), such as PyCharm. As a beginner, however, that's probably less suitable; our recommendations are equally powerful, but a lot simpler.

Our suggestions are below, but feel free to ask your coach what their preferences are – it'll be easier to get help from them.

Gedit

Gedit is an open-source, free editor, available for all operating systems.

Download it here

Sublime Text 3

Sublime Text is a very popular editor with a free evaluation period. It's easy to install and use, and it's available for all operating systems.

Download it here

Atom

Atom is an extremely new code editor created by GitHub. It's free, open-source, easy to install and easy to use. It's available for Windows, OS X and Linux.

Download it here

Why are we installing a code editor?

You might be wondering why we are installing this special code editor software, rather than using something like Word or Notepad.

The first reason is that code needs to be **plain text**, and the problem with programs like Word and Textedit is that they don't actually produce plain text, they produce rich text (with fonts and formatting), using custom formats like RTF (Rich Text Format).

The second reason is that code editors are specialized for editing code, so they can provide helpful features like highlighting code with color according to its meaning, or automatically closing quotes for you.

We'll see all this in action later. Soon, you'll come to think of your trusty old code editor as one of your favorite tools. :)

Install Git

Git is a "version control system" used by a lot of programmers. This software can track changes to files over time so that you can recall specific versions later. A bit like the "track changes" feature in Microsoft Word, but much more powerful.

Installing Git

Windows

You can download Git from git-scm.com. You can hit "next" on all steps except for one; in the fifth step entitled "Adjusting your PATH environment", choose "Use Git and optional Unix tools from the Windows Command Prompt" (the bottom option). Other than that, the defaults are fine. Checkout Windows-style, commit Unix-style line endings is good.

OS X

Download Git from git-scm.com and just follow the instructions.

> Note If you are running OS X 10.6, 10.7, or 10.8, you will need to install the version of git from here: Git installer for OS X Snow Leopard

Debian or Ubuntu

command-line

```
$ sudo apt-get install git
```

Fedora (up to 21)

command-line

```
$ sudo yum install git
```

Fedora 22+

command-line

```
$ sudo dnf install git
```

openSUSE

command-line

```
$ sudo zypper install git
```

Create a GitHub account

Go to GitHub.com and sign up for a new, free user account.

Create a PythonAnywhere account

Next it's time to sign up for a free "Beginner" account on PythonAnywhere.

- www.pythonanywhere.com

  Note When choosing your username here, bear in mind that your blog's URL will take the form yourusername.pythonanywhere.com , so choose either your own nickname, or a name for what your blog is all about.

Start reading

Congratulations, you are all set up and ready to go! If you still have some time before the workshop, it would be useful to start reading a few of the beginning chapters:

- How the internet works

- Introduction to the command line

- Introduction to Python

- What is Django?

Enjoy the workshop!

When you begin the workshop, you'll be able to go straight to Your first Django project! because you already covered the material in the earlier chapters.

How the Internet works

For readers at home: this chapter is covered in the How the Internet Works video.

This chapter is inspired by the talk "How the Internet works" by Jessica McKellar (http://web.mit.edu/jesstess/www/).

We bet you use the Internet every day. But do you actually know what happens when you type an address like https://djangogirls.org into your browser and press `enter` ?

The first thing you need to understand is that a website is just a bunch of files saved on a hard disk. Just like your movies, music, or pictures. However, there is one part that is unique for websites: they include computer code called HTML.

If you're not familiar with programming it can be hard to grasp HTML at first, but your web browsers (like Chrome, Safari, Firefox, etc.) love it. Web browsers are designed to understand this code, follow its instructions, and present these files that your website is made of, exactly the way you want.

As with every file, we need to store HTML files somewhere on a hard disk. For the Internet, we use special, powerful computers called *servers*. They don't have a screen, mouse or a keyboard, because their main purpose is to store data and serve it. That's why they're called *servers* – because they *serve* you data.

OK, but you want to know how the Internet looks, right?

We drew you a picture! It looks like this:

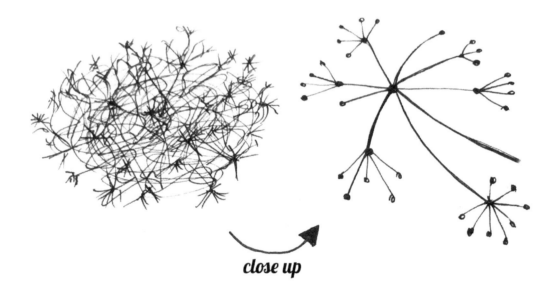

close up

Looks like a mess, right? In fact it is a network of connected machines (the above-mentioned *servers*). Hundreds of thousands of machines! Many, many kilometers of cables around the world! You can visit a Submarine Cable Map website (http://submarinecablemap.com) to see how complicated the net is. Here is a screenshot from the website:

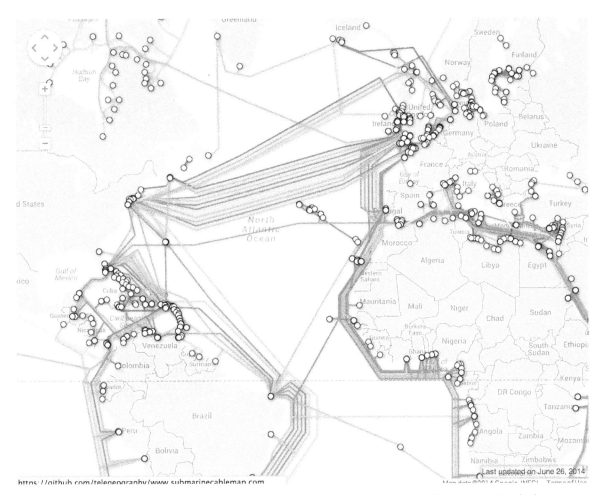

It is fascinating, isn't it? But obviously, it is not possible to have a wire between every machine connected to the Internet. So, to reach a machine (for example, the one where https://djangogirls.org is saved) we need to pass a request through many, many different machines.

It looks like this:

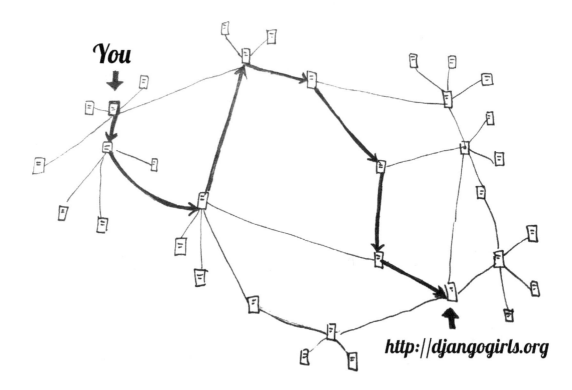

Imagine that when you type https://djangogirls.org, you send a letter that says: "Dear Django Girls, I want to see the djangogirls.org website. Send it to me, please!"

Your letter goes to the post office closest to you. Then it goes to another that is a bit nearer to your addressee, then to another, and another until it is delivered at its destination. The only unique thing is that if you send many letters (*data packets*) to the same place, they could go through totally different post offices (*routers*). This depends on how they are distributed at each office.

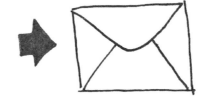

Yes, it is as simple as that. You send messages and you expect some response. Of course, instead of paper and pen you use bytes of data, but the idea is the same!

Instead of addresses with a street name, city, zip code and country name, we use IP addresses. Your computer first asks the DNS (Domain Name System) to translate djangogirls.org into an IP address. It works a little bit like old-fashioned phonebooks where you can look up the name of the person you want to contact and find their phone number and address.

When you send a letter, it needs to have certain features to be delivered correctly: an address, a stamp, etc. You also use a language that the receiver understands, right? The same applies to the *data packets* you send to see a website. We use a protocol called HTTP (Hypertext Transfer Protocol).

So, basically, when you have a website, you need to have a *server* (machine) where it lives. When the *server* receives an incoming *request* (in a letter), it sends back your website (in another letter).

Since this is a Django tutorial, you might ask what Django does. When you send a response, you don't always want to send the same thing to everybody. It is so much better if your letters are personalized, especially for the person that has just written to you, right? Django helps you with creating these personalized, interesting letters. :)

Enough talk – time to create!

Introduction to the command-line interface

For readers at home: this chapter is covered in the Your new friend: Command Line video.

It's exciting, right?! You'll write your first line of code in just a few minutes! :)

Let us introduce you to your first new friend: the command line!

The following steps will show you how to use the black window all hackers use. It might look a bit scary at first but really it's just a prompt waiting for commands from you.

Note Please note that throughout this book we use the terms 'directory' and 'folder' interchangeably but they are one and the same thing.

What is the command line?

The window, which is usually called the **command line** or **command-line interface**, is a text-based application for viewing, handling, and manipulating files on your computer. It's much like Windows Explorer or Finder on the Mac, but without the graphical interface. Other names for the command line are: *cmd, CLI, prompt, console* or *terminal*.

Open the command-line interface

To start some experiments we need to open our command-line interface first.

Windows

Go to Start menu → All Programs → Accessories → Command Prompt.

OS X

Go to Applications → Utilities → Terminal.

Linux

It's probably under Applications → Accessories → Terminal, but that may depend on your system. If it's not there, just Google it. :)

Prompt

You now should see a white or black window that is waiting for your commands.

OS X and Linux

If you're on Mac or Linux, you probably see $, just like this:

command-line

```
$
```

Windows

On Windows, it's a `>` sign, like this:

command-line

```
>
```

Each command will be prepended by this sign and one space, but you don't have to type it. Your computer will do it for you. :)

> Just a small note: in your case there may be something like `C:\Users\ola>` or `Olas-MacBook-Air:~ ola$` before the prompt sign, and this is 100% OK.

The part up to and including the `$` or the `>` is called the *command line prompt*, or *prompt* for short. It prompts you to input something there.

In the tutorial, when we want you to type in a command, we will include the `$` or `>`, and occasionally more to the left. You can ignore the left part and just type in the command which starts after the prompt.

Your first command (YAY!)

Let's start with something simple. Type this command:

OS X and Linux

command-line

```
$ whoami
```

Windows

command-line

```
> whoami
```

And then hit `enter`. This is our result:

command-line

```
$ whoami
olasitarska
```

As you can see, the computer has just printed your username. Neat, huh? :)

> Try to type each command; do not copy-paste. You'll remember more this way!

Basics

Each operating system has a slightly different set of commands for the command line, so make sure to follow instructions for your operating system. Let's try this, shall we?

Current directory

It'd be nice to know where are we now, right? Let's see. Type this command and hit `enter` :

OS X and Linux

command-line

```
$ pwd
/Users/olasitarska
```

Note: 'pwd' stands for 'print working directory'.

Windows

command-line

```
> cd
C:\Users\olasitarska
```

Note: 'cd' stands for 'change directory'. With powershell you can use pwd just like on Linux or Mac OS X.

You'll probably see something similar on your machine. Once you open the command line you usually start at your user's home directory.

List files and directories

So what's in it? It'd be cool to find out. Let's see:

OS X and Linux

command-line

```
$ ls
Applications
Desktop
Downloads
Music
...
```

Windows

command-line

```
> dir
 Directory of C:\Users\olasitarska
05/08/2014 07:28 PM <DIR>     Applications
05/08/2014 07:28 PM <DIR>     Desktop
05/08/2014 07:28 PM <DIR>     Downloads
05/08/2014 07:28 PM <DIR>     Music
...
```

Change current directory

Now, let's go to our Desktop directory:

OS X and Linux

command-line

```
$ cd Desktop
```

Windows

command-line

```
> cd Desktop
```

Check if it's really changed:

OS X and Linux

command-line

```
$ pwd
/Users/olasitarska/Desktop
```

Windows

command-line

```
> cd
C:\Users\olasitarska\Desktop
```

Here it is!

> PRO tip: if you type cd D and then hit tab on your keyboard, the command line will automatically fill in the rest of the name so you can navigate faster. If there is more than one folder starting with "D", hit the tab key twice to get a list of options.

Create directory

How about creating a practice directory on your desktop? You can do it this way:

OS X and Linux

command-line

```
$ mkdir practice
```

Windows

command-line

```
> mkdir practice
```

This little command will create a folder with the name `practice` on your desktop. You can check if it's there just by looking on your Desktop or by running a `ls` or `dir` command! Try it. :)

> PRO tip: If you don't want to type the same commands over and over, try pressing the `up arrow` and `down arrow` on your keyboard to cycle through recently used commands.

Exercise!

A small challenge for you: in your newly created `practice` directory, create a directory called `test` . (Use the `cd` and `mkdir` commands.)

Solution:

OS X and Linux

command-line

```
$ cd practice
$ mkdir test
$ ls
test
```

Windows

command-line

```
> cd practice
> mkdir test
> dir
05/08/2014 07:28 PM <DIR>        test
```

Congrats! :)

Clean up

We don't want to leave a mess, so let's remove everything we did until that point.

First, we need to get back to Desktop:

OS X and Linux

command-line

```
$ cd ..
```

Windows

command-line

```
> cd ..
```

Using `..` with the `cd` command will change your current directory to the parent directory (that is, the directory that contains your current directory).

Check where you are:

OS X and Linux

command-line

```
$ pwd
/Users/olasitarska/Desktop
```

Windows

command-line

```
> cd
C:\Users\olasitarska\Desktop
```

Now time to delete the `practice` directory:

> Attention: Deleting files using `del`, `rmdir` or `rm` is irrecoverable, meaning *the deleted files will be gone forever!* So be very careful with this command.

OS X and Linux

command-line

```
$ rm -r practice
```

Windows

command-line

```
> rmdir /S practice
practice, Are you sure <Y/N>? Y
```

Done! To be sure it's actually deleted, let's check it:

OS X and Linux

command-line

```
$ ls
```

Windows

command-line

```
> dir
```

Exit

That's it for now! You can safely close the command line now. Let's do it the hacker way, alright? :)

OS X and Linux

command-line

```
$ exit
```

Windows

command-line

```
> exit
```

Cool, huh? :)

Summary

Here is a summary of some useful commands:

Command (Windows)	Command (Mac OS / Linux)	Description	Example
exit	exit	close the window	**exit**
cd	cd	change directory	**cd test**
cd	pwd	show the current directory	**cd** (Windows) or **pwd** (Mac OS / Linux)
dir	ls	list directories/files	**dir**
copy	cp	copy file	**copy c:\test\test.txt c:\windows\test.txt**
move	mv	move file	**move c:\test\test.txt c:\windows\test.txt**
mkdir	mkdir	create a new directory	**mkdir testdirectory**
rmdir (or del)	rm	delete a file	**del c:\test\test.txt**
rmdir /S	rm -r	delete a directory	**rm -r testdirectory**

These are just a very few of the commands you can run in your command line, but you're not going to use anything more than that today.

If you're curious, ss64.com contains a complete reference of commands for all operating systems.

Ready?

Let's dive into Python!

Let's start with Python

We're finally here!

But first, let us tell you what Python is. Python is a very popular programming language that can be used for creating websites, games, scientific software, graphics, and much, much more.

Python originated in the late 1980s and its main goal is to be readable by human beings (not only machines!). This is why it looks much simpler than other programming languages. This makes it easy to learn, but don't worry – Python is also really powerful!

Python installation

Note If you're using a Chromebook, skip this chapter and make sure you follow the Chromebook Setup instructions.

Note If you already worked through the Installation steps, there's no need to do this again – you can skip straight ahead to the next chapter!

For readers at home: this chapter is covered in the Installing Python & Code Editor video.

This section is based on a tutorial by Geek Girls Carrots (https://github.com/ggcarrots/django-carrots)

Django is written in Python. We need Python to do anything in Django. Let's start by installing it! We want you to install Python 3.5, so if you have any earlier version, you will need to upgrade it.

Windows

First check whether your computer is running a 32-bit version or a 64-bit version of Windows at https://support.microsoft.com/en-au/kb/827218. You can download Python for Windows from the website https://www.python.org/downloads/windows/. Click on the "Latest Python 3 Release - Python x.x.x" link. If your computer is running a **64-bit** version of Windows, download the **Windows x86-64 executable installer**. Otherwise, download the **Windows x86 executable installer**. After downloading the installer, you should run it (double-click on it) and follow the instructions there.

One thing to watch out for: During the installation you will notice a window marked "Setup". Make sure you tick the "Add Python 3.5 to PATH" checkbox and click on "Install Now", as shown here:

Python 3.5.1 (64-bit) Setup   —   ✕

Install Python 3.5.1 (64-bit)

Select Install Now to install Python with default settings, or choose Customize to enable or disable features.

→ Install Now
C:\Users\Username\AppData\Local\Programs\Python\Python35

Includes IDLE, pip and documentation
Creates shortcuts and file associations

→ Customize installation
Choose location and features

☐ Install launcher for all users (recommended)

☑ Add Python 3.5 to PATH   Cancel

In upcoming steps, you'll be using the Windows Command Line (which we'll also tell you about). For now, if you need to type in some commands, go to Start menu → All Programs → Accessories → Command Prompt. You can also hold in the Windows key and press the "R"-key until the "Run" window pops up. To open the Command Line, type "cmd" and press enter in the "Run" window. (On newer versions of Windows, you might have to search for "Command Prompt" since it's sometimes hidden.)

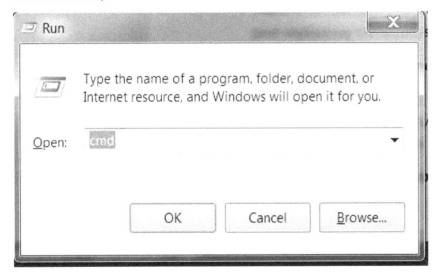

Note: if you are using an older version of Windows (7, Vista, or any older version) and the Python 3.5.x installer fails with an error, you can try either:

1. install all Windows Updates and try to install Python 3.5 again; or
2. install an older version of Python, e.g., 3.4.4.

If you install an older version of Python, the installation screen may look a bit different than shown above. Make sure you scroll down to see "Add python.exe to Path", then click the button on the left and pick "Will be installed on local hard drive":

OS X

You need to go to the website https://www.python.org/downloads/release/python-351/ and download the Python installer:

- Download the *Mac OS X 64-bit/32-bit installer* file,
- Double click *python-3.5.1-macosx10.6.pkg* to run the installer.

Linux

It is very likely that you already have Python installed out of the box. To check if you have it installed (and which version it is), open a console and type the following command:

command-line

```
$ python3 --version
Python 3.5.1
```

If you have a different 'micro version' of Python installed, e.g. 3.5.0, then you don't have to upgrade. If you don't have Python installed, or if you want a different version, you can install it as follows:

Debian or Ubuntu

Type this command into your console:

command-line

```
$ sudo apt-get install python3.5
```

Fedora (up to 21)

Use this command in your console:

command-line

```
$ sudo yum install python3
```

Fedora (22+)

Use this command in your console:

command-line

```
$ sudo dnf install python3
```

openSUSE

Use this command in your console:

command-line

```
$ sudo zypper install python3
```

Verify the installation was successful by opening the *Terminal* application and running the `python3` command:

command-line

```
$ python3 --version
Python 3.5.1
```

NOTE: If you're on Windows and you get an error message that `python3` wasn't found, try using `python` (without the `3`) and check if it still might be a version of Python 3.5.

If you have any doubts, or if something went wrong and you have no idea what to do next, please ask your coach! Sometimes things don't go smoothly and it's better to ask for help from someone with more experience.

Code editor

For readers at home: this chapter is covered in the Installing Python & Code Editor video.

You're about to write your first line of code, so it's time to download a code editor!

If you're using a Chromebook, skip this chapter and make sure you follow the Chromebook Setup instructions.

Note You might have done this earlier in the Installation chapter – if so, you can skip right ahead to the next chapter!

There are a lot of different editors and it largely boils down to personal preference. Most Python programmers use complex but extremely powerful IDEs (Integrated Development Environments), such as PyCharm. As a beginner, however, that's probably less suitable; our recommendations are equally powerful, but a lot simpler.

Our suggestions are below, but feel free to ask your coach what their preferences are – it'll be easier to get help from them.

Gedit

Gedit is an open-source, free editor, available for all operating systems.

Download it here

Sublime Text 3

Sublime Text is a very popular editor with a free evaluation period. It's easy to install and use, and it's available for all operating systems.

Download it here

Atom

Atom is an extremely new code editor created by GitHub. It's free, open-source, easy to install and easy to use. It's available for Windows, OS X and Linux.

Download it here

Why are we installing a code editor?

You might be wondering why we are installing this special code editor software, rather than using something like Word or Notepad.

The first reason is that code needs to be **plain text**, and the problem with programs like Word and Textedit is that they don't actually produce plain text, they produce rich text (with fonts and formatting), using custom formats like RTF (Rich Text Format).

The second reason is that code editors are specialized for editing code, so they can provide helpful features like highlighting code with color according to its meaning, or automatically closing quotes for you.

We'll see all this in action later. Soon, you'll come to think of your trusty old code editor as one of your favorite tools. :)

Introduction to Python

Part of this chapter is based on tutorials by Geek Girls Carrots (https://github.com/ggcarrots/django-carrots).

Let's write some code!

Python prompt

For readers at home: this part is covered in the Python Basics: Integers, Strings, Lists, Variables and Errors video.

To start playing with Python, we need to open up a *command line* on your computer. You should already know how to do that – you learned it in the Intro to Command Line chapter.

Once you're ready, follow the instructions below.

We want to open up a Python console, so type in `python` on Windows or `python3` on Mac OS/Linux and hit `enter` .

command-line

```
$ python3
Python 3.5.1 (...)
Type "help", "copyright", "credits" or "license" for more information.
>>>
```

Your first Python command!

After running the Python command, the prompt changed to `>>>` . For us this means that for now we may only use commands in the Python language. You don't have to type in `>>>` – Python will do that for you.

If you want to exit the Python console at any point, just type `exit()` or use the shortcut `Ctrl + Z` for Windows and `Ctrl + D` for Mac/Linux. Then you won't see `>>>` any longer.

For now, we don't want to exit the Python console. We want to learn more about it. Let's start with something really simple. For example, try typing some math, like `2 + 3` and hit `enter` .

command-line

```
>>> 2 + 3
5
```

Nice! See how the answer popped out? Python knows math! You could try other commands like:

- `4 * 5`
- `5 - 1`
- `40 / 2`

To perform exponential calculation, say 2 to the power 3, we type:

command-line

```
>>> 2 ** 3
8
```

Have fun with this for a little while and then get back here. :)

As you can see, Python is a great calculator. If you're wondering what else you can do…

Strings

How about your name? Type your first name in quotes like this:

command-line

```
>>> "Ola"
'Ola'
```

You've now created your first string! It's a sequence of characters that can be processed by a computer. The string must always begin and end with the same character. This may be single (') or double (") quotes (there is no difference!) The quotes tell Python that what's inside of them is a string.

Strings can be strung together. Try this:

command-line

```
>>> "Hi there " + "Ola"
'Hi there Ola'
```

You can also multiply strings with a number:

command-line

```
>>> "Ola" * 3
'OlaOlaOla'
```

If you need to put an apostrophe inside your string, you have two ways to do it.

Using double quotes:

command-line

```
>>> "Runnin' down the hill"
"Runnin' down the hill"
```

or escaping the apostrophe with a backslash (\ ):

command-line

```
>>> 'Runnin\' down the hill'
"Runnin' down the hill"
```

Nice, huh? To see your name in uppercase letters, simply type:

command-line

```
>>> "Ola".upper()
'OLA'
```

You just used the `upper` **method** on your string! A method (like `upper()`) is a sequence of instructions that Python has to perform on a given object (`"Ola"`) once you call it.

If you want to know the number of letters contained in your name, there is a **function** for that too!

command-line

```
>>> len("Ola")
3
```

Wonder why sometimes you call functions with a `.` at the end of a string (like `"Ola".upper()`) and sometimes you first call a function and place the string in parentheses? Well, in some cases, functions belong to objects, like `upper()`, which can only be performed on strings. In this case, we call the function a **method**. Other times, functions don't belong to anything specific and can be used on different types of objects, just like `len()`. That's why we're giving `"Ola"` as a parameter to the `len` function.

Summary

OK, enough of strings. So far you've learned about:

- **the prompt** – typing commands (code) into the Python prompt results in answers in Python
- **numbers and strings** – in Python numbers are used for math and strings for text objects
- **operators** – like `+` and `*` , combine values to produce a new one
- **functions** – like `upper()` and `len()` , perform actions on objects.

These are the basics of every programming language you learn. Ready for something harder? We bet you are!

Errors

Let's try something new. Can we get the length of a number the same way we could find out the length of our name? Type in `len(304023)` and hit `enter` :

command-line

```
>>> len(304023)
Traceback (most recent call last):
  File "<stdin>", line 1, in <module>
TypeError: object of type 'int' has no len()
```

We got our first error! It says that objects of type "int" (integers, whole numbers) have no length. So what can we do now? Maybe we can write our number as a string? Strings have a length, right?

command-line

```
>>> len(str(304023))
6
```

It worked! We used the `str` function inside of the `len` function. `str()` converts everything to strings.

- The `str` function converts things into **strings**
- The `int` function converts things into **integers**

> Important: we can convert numbers into text, but we can't necessarily convert text into numbers – what would `int('hello')` be anyway?

Variables

An important concept in programming is variables. A variable is nothing more than a name for something so you can use it later. Programmers use these variables to store data, make their code more readable and so they don't have to keep remembering what things are.

Let's say we want to create a new variable called `name` :

command-line

```
>>> name = "Ola"
```

You see? It's easy! It's simply: name equals Ola.

As you've noticed, your program didn't return anything like it did before. So how do we know that the variable actually exists? Simply enter `name` and hit `enter` :

command-line

```
>>> name
'Ola'
```

Yippee! Your first variable! :) You can always change what it refers to:

command-line

```
>>> name = "Sonja"
>>> name
'Sonja'
```

You can use it in functions too:

command-line

```
>>> len(name)
5
```

Awesome, right? Of course, variables can be anything – numbers too! Try this:

command-line

```
>>> a = 4
>>> b = 6
>>> a * b
24
```

But what if we used the wrong name? Can you guess what would happen? Let's try!

command-line

```
>>> city = "Tokyo"
>>> ctiy
Traceback (most recent call last):
  File "<stdin>", line 1, in <module>
NameError: name 'ctiy' is not defined
```

An error! As you can see, Python has different types of errors and this one is called a **NameError**. Python will give you this error if you try to use a variable that hasn't been defined yet. If you encounter this error later, check your code to see if you've mistyped any names.

Play with this for a while and see what you can do!

The print function

Try this:

command-line

```
>>> name = 'Maria'
>>> name
'Maria'
>>> print(name)
Maria
```

When you just type `name`, the Python interpreter responds with the string *representation* of the variable 'name', which is the letters M-a-r-i-a, surrounded by single quotes, ''. When you say `print(name)`, Python will "print" the contents of the variable to the screen, without the quotes, which is neater.

As we'll see later, `print()` is also useful when we want to print things from inside functions, or when we want to print things on multiple lines.

Lists

Beside strings and integers, Python has all sorts of different types of objects. Now we're going to introduce one called **list**. Lists are exactly what you think they are: objects which are lists of other objects. :)

Go ahead and create a list:

command-line

```
>>> []
[]
```

Yes, this list is empty. Not very useful, right? Let's create a list of lottery numbers. We don't want to repeat ourselves all the time, so we will put it in a variable, too:

command-line

```
>>> lottery = [3, 42, 12, 19, 30, 59]
```

All right, we have a list! What can we do with it? Let's see how many lottery numbers there are in a list. Do you have any idea which function you should use for that? You know this already!

command-line

```
>>> len(lottery)
6
```

Yes! `len()` can give you a number of objects in a list. Handy, right? Maybe we will sort it now:

command-line

```
>>> lottery.sort()
```

This doesn't return anything, it just changed the order in which the numbers appear in the list. Let's print it out again and see what happened:

command-line

```
>>> print(lottery)
[3, 12, 19, 30, 42, 59]
```

As you can see, the numbers in your list are now sorted from the lowest to highest value. Congrats!

Maybe we want to reverse that order? Let's do that!

command-line

```
>>> lottery.reverse()
>>> print(lottery)
[59, 42, 30, 19, 12, 3]
```

Easy, right? If you want to add something to your list, you can do this by typing this command:

command-line

```
>>> lottery.append(199)
>>> print(lottery)
[59, 42, 30, 19, 12, 3, 199]
```

If you want to show only the first number, you can do this by using **indexes**. An index is the number that says where in a list an item occurs. Programmers prefer to start counting at 0, so the first object in your list is at index 0, the next one is at 1, and so on. Try this:

command-line

```
>>> print(lottery[0])
59
>>> print(lottery[1])
42
```

As you can see, you can access different objects in your list by using the list's name and the object's index inside of square brackets.

To delete something from your list you will need to use **indexes** as we learned above and the `pop()` method. Let's try an example and reinforce what we learned previously; we will be deleting the first number of our list.

command-line

```
>>> print(lottery)
[59, 42, 30, 19, 12, 3, 199]
>>> print(lottery[0])
59
>>> lottery.pop(0)
59
>>> print(lottery)
[42, 30, 19, 12, 3, 199]
```

That worked like a charm!

For extra fun, try some other indexes: 6, 7, 1000, -1, -6 or -1000. See if you can predict the result before trying the command. Do the results make sense?

You can find a list of all available list methods in this chapter of the Python documentation:
https://docs.python.org/3/tutorial/datastructures.html

Dictionaries

For readers at home, this part is covered in the Python Basics: Dictionaries video.

A dictionary is similar to a list, but you access values by looking up a key instead of a numeric index. A key can be any string or number. The syntax to define an empty dictionary is:

command-line

```
>>> {}
{}
```

This shows that you just created an empty dictionary. Hurray!

Now, try writing the following command (try substituting your own information, too):

command-line

```
>>> participant = {'name': 'Ola', 'country': 'Poland', 'favorite_numbers': [7, 42, 92]}
```

With this command, you just created a variable named `participant` with three key–value pairs:

- The key `name` points to the value `'Ola'` (a `string` object),
- `country` points to `'Poland'` (another `string`),
- and `favorite_numbers` points to `[7, 42, 92]` (a `list` with three numbers in it).

You can check the content of individual keys with this syntax:

command-line

```
>>> print(participant['name'])
Ola
```

See, it's similar to a list. But you don't need to remember the index – just the name.

What happens if we ask Python the value of a key that doesn't exist? Can you guess? Let's try it and see!

command-line

```
>>> participant['age']
Traceback (most recent call last):
  File "<stdin>", line 1, in <module>
KeyError: 'age'
```

Look, another error! This one is a **KeyError**. Python is helpful and tells you that the key `'age'` doesn't exist in this dictionary.

When should you use a dictionary or a list? Well, that's a good point to ponder. Just have a solution in mind before looking at the answer in the next line.

- Do you just need an ordered sequence of items? Go for a list.
- Do you need to associate values with keys, so you can look them up efficiently (by key) later on? Use a dictionary.

Dictionaries, like lists, are *mutable*, meaning that they can be changed after they are created. You can add new key–value pairs to a dictionary after it is created, like this:

command-line

```
>>> participant['favorite_language'] = 'Python'
```

Like lists, using the `len()` method on the dictionaries returns the number of key–value pairs in the dictionary. Go ahead and type in this command:

command-line

```
>>> len(participant)
4
```

I hope it makes sense up to now. :) Ready for some more fun with dictionaries? Read on for some amazing things.

You can use the `pop()` method to delete an item in the dictionary. Say, if you want to delete the entry corresponding to the key `'favorite_numbers'` , just type in the following command:

command-line

```
>>> participant.pop('favorite_numbers')
[7, 42, 92]
>>> participant
{'country': 'Poland', 'favorite_language': 'Python', 'name': 'Ola'}
```

As you can see from the output, the key–value pair corresponding to the 'favorite_numbers' key has been deleted.

As well as this, you can also change a value associated with an already-created key in the dictionary. Type this:

command-line

```
>>> participant['country'] = 'Germany'
>>> participant
{'country': 'Germany', 'favorite_language': 'Python', 'name': 'Ola'}
```

As you can see, the value of the key `'country'` has been altered from `'Poland'` to `'Germany'` . :) Exciting? Hurrah! You just learned another amazing thing.

Summary

Awesome! You know a lot about programming now. In this last part you learned about:

- **errors** – you now know how to read and understand errors that show up if Python doesn't understand a command you've given it
- **variables** – names for objects that allow you to code more easily and to make your code more readable
- **lists** – lists of objects stored in a particular order
- **dictionaries** – objects stored as key–value pairs

Excited for the next part? :)

Compare things

For readers at home: this part is covered in the Python Basics: Comparisons video.

A big part of programming involves comparing things. What's the easiest thing to compare? Numbers, of course. Let's see how that works:

command-line

```
>>> 5 > 2
True
>>> 3 < 1
False
>>> 5 > 2 * 2
True
>>> 1 == 1
True
>>> 5 != 2
True
```

We gave Python some numbers to compare. As you can see, not only can Python compare numbers, but it can also compare method results. Nice, huh?

Do you wonder why we put two equal signs `==` next to each other to compare if numbers are equal? We use a single `=` for assigning values to variables. You always, **always** need to put two of them – `==` – if you want to check if things are equal to each other. We can also state that things are unequal to each other. For that, we use the symbol `!=`, as shown in the example above.

Give Python two more tasks:

command-line

```
>>> 6 >= 12 / 2
True
>>> 3 <= 2
False
```

`>` and `<` are easy, but what do `>=` and `<=` mean? Read them like this:

- `x > y` means: x is greater than y
- `x < y` means: x is less than y
- `x <= y` means: x is less than or equal to y
- `x >= y` means: x is greater than or equal to y

Awesome! Wanna do one more? Try this:

command-line

```
>>> 6 > 2 and 2 < 3
True
>>> 3 > 2 and 2 < 1
False
>>> 3 > 2 or 2 < 1
True
```

You can give Python as many numbers to compare as you want, and it will give you an answer! Pretty smart, right?

- **and** – if you use the `and` operator, both comparisons have to be True in order for the whole command to be True
- **or** – if you use the `or` operator, only one of the comparisons has to be True in order for the whole command to be True

Have you heard of the expression "comparing apples to oranges"? Let's try the Python equivalent:

command-line

```
>>> 1 > 'django'
Traceback (most recent call last):
  File "<stdin>", line 1, in <module>
TypeError: unorderable types: int() > str()
```

Here you see that just like in the expression, Python is not able to compare a number (`int`) and a string (`str`). Instead, it shows a **TypeError** and tells us the two types can't be compared together.

Boolean

Incidentally, you just learned about a new type of object in Python. It's called **Boolean**, and it is probably the easiest type there is.

There are only two Boolean objects:

- True
- False

But for Python to understand this, you need to always write it as 'True' (first letter uppercase, with the rest of the letters lowercased). **true, TRUE, and tRUE won't work – only True is correct.** (The same applies to 'False' as well, of course.)

Booleans can be variables, too! See here:

command-line

```
>>> a = True
>>> a
True
```

You can also do it this way:

command-line

```
>>> a = 2 > 5
>>> a
False
```

Practice and have fun with Booleans by trying to run the following commands:

- `True and True`
- `False and True`
- `True or 1 == 1`
- `1 != 2`

Congrats! Booleans are one of the coolest features in programming, and you just learned how to use them!

Save it!

For readers at home: this part is covered in the Python Basics: Saving files and "If" statement video.

So far we've been writing all our python code in the interpreter, which limits us to entering one line of code at a time. Normal programs are saved in files and executed by our programming language **interpreter** or **compiler**. So far we've been running our programs one line at a time in the Python **interpreter**. We're going to need more than one line of code for the next few tasks, so we'll quickly need to:

- Exit the Python interpreter
- Open up our code editor of choice
- Save some code into a new python file
- Run it!

To exit from the Python interpreter that we've been using, simply type the `exit()` function

command-line

```
>>> exit()
$
```

This will put you back into the command prompt.

Earlier, we picked out a code editor from the code editor section. We'll need to open the editor now and write some code into a new file:

editor

```
print('Hello, Django girls!')
```

Obviously, you're a pretty seasoned Python developer now, so feel free to write some code that you've learned today.

Now we need to save the file and give it a descriptive name. Let's call the file **python_intro.py** and save it to your desktop. We can name the file anything we want, but the important part here is to make sure the file ends in **.py**. The **.py** extension tells our operating system that this is a **Python executable file** and Python can run it.

> **Note** You should notice one of the coolest thing about code editors: colors! In the Python console, everything was the same color; now you should see that the `print` function is a different color from the string. This is called "syntax highlighting", and it's a really useful feature when coding. The color of things will give you hints, such as unclosed strings or a typo in a keyword name (like the `def` in a function, which we'll see below). This is one of the reasons we use a code editor. :)

With the file saved, it's time to run it! Using the skills you've learned in the command line section, use the terminal to **change directories** to the desktop.

OS X

On a Mac, the command will look something like this:

command-line

```
$ cd ~/Desktop
```

Linux

On Linux, it will be like this (the word "Desktop" might be translated to your local language):

command-line

```
$ cd ~/Desktop
```

Windows

And on Windows, it will be like this:

command-line

```
> cd %HomePath%\Desktop
```

If you get stuck, just ask for help.

Now use Python to execute the code in the file like this:

command-line

```
$ python3 python_intro.py
Hello, Django girls!
```

Note: on Windows 'python3' is not recognized as a command. Instead, use 'python' to execute the file:

command-line

```
> python python_intro.py
```

Alright! You just ran your first Python program that was saved to a file. Feel awesome?

You can now move on to an essential tool in programming:

If ... elif ... else

Lots of things in code should be executed only when given conditions are met. That's why Python has something called **if statements**.

Replace the code in your **python_intro.py** file with this:

python_intro.py

```
if 3 > 2:
```

If we were to save and run this, we'd see an error like this:

command-line

```
$ python3 python_intro.py
  File "python_intro.py", line 2
                                 ^
SyntaxError: unexpected EOF while parsing
```

Python expects us to give further instructions to it which are executed if the condition `3 > 2` turns out to be true (or `True` for that matter). Let's try to make Python print "It works!". Change your code in your **python_intro.py** file to this:

python_intro.py

```
if 3 > 2:
    print('It works!')
```

Notice how we've indented the next line of code by 4 spaces? We need to do this so Python knows what code to run if the result is true. You can do one space, but nearly all Python programmers do 4 to make things look neat. A single `tab` will also count as 4 spaces.

Save it and give it another run:

command-line

```
$ python3 python_intro.py
It works!
```

Note: Remember that on Windows, 'python3' is not recognized as a command. From now on, replace 'python3' with 'python' to execute the file.

What if a condition isn't True?

In previous examples, code was executed only when the conditions were True. But Python also has `elif` and `else` statements:

python_intro.py

```
if 5 > 2:
    print('5 is indeed greater than 2')
else:
    print('5 is not greater than 2')
```

When this is run it will print out:

command-line

```
$ python3 python_intro.py
5 is indeed greater than 2
```

If 2 were a greater number than 5, then the second command would be executed. Easy, right? Let's see how `elif` works:

python_intro.py

```
name = 'Sonja'
if name == 'Ola':
    print('Hey Ola!')
elif name == 'Sonja':
    print('Hey Sonja!')
else:
    print('Hey anonymous!')
```

and executed:

command-line

```
$ python3 python_intro.py
Hey Sonja!
```

See what happened there? `elif` lets you add extra conditions that run if the previous conditions fail.

You can add as many `elif` statements as you like after your initial `if` statement. For example:

python_intro.py

```
volume = 57
if volume < 20:
    print("It's kinda quiet.")
elif 20 <= volume < 40:
    print("It's nice for background music")
elif 40 <= volume < 60:
    print("Perfect, I can hear all the details")
elif 60 <= volume < 80:
    print("Nice for parties")
elif 80 <= volume < 100:
    print("A bit loud!")
else:
    print("My ears are hurting! :(")
```

Python runs through each test in sequence and prints:

command-line

```
$ python3 python_intro.py
Perfect, I can hear all the details
```

Comments

Comments are lines beginning with `#` . You can write whatever you want after the `#` and Python will ignore it. Comments can make your code easier for other people to understand.

Let's see how that looks:

python_intro.py

```
# Change the volume if it's too loud or too quiet
if volume < 20 or volume > 80:
    volume = 50
    print("That's better!")
```

You don't need to write a comment for every line of code, but they are useful for explaining why your code is doing something, or providing a summary when it's doing something complex.

Summary

In the last few exercises you learned about:

- **comparing things** – in Python you can compare things by using `>` , `>=` , `==` , `<=` , `<` and the `and` , `or` operators
- **Boolean** – a type of object that can only have one of two values: `True` or `False`
- **Saving files** – storing code in files so you can execute larger programs.
- **if ... elif ... else** – statements that allow you to execute code only when certain conditions are met.
- **comments** - lines that Python won't run which let you document your code

Time for the last part of this chapter!

Your own functions!

For readers at home: this part is covered in the Python Basics: Functions video.

Remember functions like `len()` that you can execute in Python? Well, good news – you will learn how to write your own functions now!

A function is a sequence of instructions that Python should execute. Each function in Python starts with the keyword `def` , is given a name, and can have some parameters. Let's start with an easy one. Replace the code in **python_intro.py** with the following:

python_intro.py

```
def hi():
    print('Hi there!')
    print('How are you?')

hi()
```

Okay, our first function is ready!

You may wonder why we've written the name of the function at the bottom of the file. This is because Python reads the file and executes it from top to bottom. So in order to use our function, we have to re-write it at the bottom.

Let's run this now and see what happens:

command-line

```
$ python3 python_intro.py
Hi there!
How are you?
```

Note: if it didn't work, don't panic! The output will help you to figure why:

- If you get a `NameError` , that probably means you typed something wrong, so you should check that you used the same name when creating the function with `def hi():` and when calling it with `hi()` .
- If you get an `IndentationError` , check that both of the `print` lines have the same whitespace at the start of a line: python wants all the code inside the function to be neatly aligned.
- If there's no output at all, check that the last `hi()` *isn't* indented - if it is, that line will become part of the function too,

and it will never get run.

Let's build our first function with parameters. We will use the previous example – a function that says 'hi' to the person running it – with a name:

python_intro.py

```python
def hi(name):
```

As you can see, we now gave our function a parameter that we called `name` :

python_intro.py

```python
def hi(name):
    if name == 'Ola':
        print('Hi Ola!')
    elif name == 'Sonja':
        print('Hi Sonja!')
    else:
        print('Hi anonymous!')

hi()
```

Remember: The `print` function is indented four spaces within the `if` statement. This is because the function runs when the condition is met. Let's see how it works now:

command-line

```
$ python3 python_intro.py
Traceback (most recent call last):
File "python_intro.py", line 10, in <module>
  hi()
TypeError: hi() missing 1 required positional argument: 'name'
```

Oops, an error. Luckily, Python gives us a pretty useful error message. It tells us that the function `hi()` (the one we defined) has one required argument (called `name`) and that we forgot to pass it when calling the function. Let's fix it at the bottom of the file:

python_intro.py

```python
hi("Ola")
```

And run it again:

command-line

```
$ python3 python_intro.py
Hi Ola!
```

And if we change the name?

python_intro.py

```python
hi("Sonja")
```

And run it:

command-line

```
$ python3 python_intro.py
Hi Sonja!
```

Now, what do you think will happen if you write another name in there? (Not Ola or Sonja.) Give it a try and see if you're right. It should print out this:

command-line

```
Hi anonymous!
```

This is awesome, right? This way you don't have to repeat yourself every time you want to change the name of the person the function is supposed to greet. And that's exactly why we need functions – you never want to repeat your code!

Let's do something smarter – there are more names than two, and writing a condition for each would be hard, right?

python_intro.py

```
def hi(name):
    print('Hi ' + name + '!')

hi("Rachel")
```

Let's call the code now:

command-line

```
$ python3 python_intro.py
Hi Rachel!
```

Congratulations! You just learned how to write functions! :)

Loops

For readers at home: this part is covered in the Python Basics: For Loop video.

This is the last part already. That was quick, right? :)

Programmers don't like to repeat themselves. Programming is all about automating things, so we don't want to greet every person by their name manually, right? That's where loops come in handy.

Still remember lists? Let's do a list of girls:

python_intro.py

```
girls = ['Rachel', 'Monica', 'Phoebe', 'Ola', 'You']
```

We want to greet all of them by their name. We have the `hi` function to do that, so let's use it in a loop:

python_intro.py

```
for name in girls:
```

The `for` statement behaves similarly to the `if` statement; code below both of these need to be indented four spaces.

Here is the full code that will be in the file:

python_intro.py

```
def hi(name):
    print('Hi ' + name + '!')

girls = ['Rachel', 'Monica', 'Phoebe', 'Ola', 'You']
for name in girls:
    hi(name)
    print('Next girl')
```

And when we run it:

command-line

```
$ python3 python_intro.py
Hi Rachel!
Next girl
Hi Monica!
Next girl
Hi Phoebe!
Next girl
Hi Ola!
Next girl
Hi You!
Next girl
```

As you can see, everything you put inside a `for` statement with an indent will be repeated for every element of the list `girls` .

You can also use `for` on numbers using the `range` function:

python_intro.py

```
for i in range(1, 6):
    print(i)
```

Which would print:

command-line

```
1
2
3
4
5
```

`range` is a function that creates a list of numbers following one after the other (these numbers are provided by you as parameters).

Note that the second of these two numbers is not included in the list that is output by Python (meaning `range(1, 6)` counts from 1 to 5, but does not include the number 6). That is because "range" is half-open, and by that we mean it includes the first value, but not the last.

Summary

That's it. **You totally rock!** This was a tricky chapter, so you should feel proud of yourself. We're definitely proud of you for making it this far!

You might want to briefly do something else – stretch, walk around for a bit, rest your eyes – before going on to the next chapter. :)

What is Django?

Django (/'dʒæŋgoʊ/ *jang-goh*) is a free and open source web application framework, written in Python. A web framework is a set of components that helps you to develop websites faster and easier.

When you're building a website, you always need a similar set of components: a way to handle user authentication (signing up, signing in, signing out), a management panel for your website, forms, a way to upload files, etc.

Luckily for you, other people long ago noticed that web developers face similar problems when building a new site, so they teamed up and created frameworks (Django being one of them) that give you ready-made components to use.

Frameworks exist to save you from having to reinvent the wheel and to help alleviate some of the overhead when you're building a new site.

Why do you need a framework?

To understand what Django is actually for, we need to take a closer look at the servers. The first thing is that the server needs to know that you want it to serve you a web page.

Imagine a mailbox (port) which is monitored for incoming letters (requests). This is done by a web server. The web server reads the letter and then sends a response with a webpage. But when you want to send something, you need to have some content. And Django is something that helps you create the content.

What happens when someone requests a website from your server?

When a request comes to a web server, it's passed to Django which tries to figure out what is actually requested. It takes a web page address first and tries to figure out what to do. This part is done by Django's **urlresolver** (note that a website address is called a URL – Uniform Resource Locator – so the name *urlresolver* makes sense). It is not very smart – it takes a list of patterns and tries to match the URL. Django checks patterns from top to bottom and if something is matched, then Django passes the request to the associated function (which is called *view*).

Imagine a mail carrier with a letter. She is walking down the street and checks each house number against the one on the letter. If it matches, she puts the letter there. This is how the urlresolver works!

In the *view* function, all the interesting things are done: we can look at a database to look for some information. Maybe the user asked to change something in the data? Like a letter saying, "Please change the description of my job." The *view* can check if you are allowed to do that, then update the job description for you and send back a message: "Done!" Then the *view* generates a response and Django can send it to the user's web browser.

Of course, the description above is a little bit simplified, but you don't need to know all the technical things yet. Having a general idea is enough.

So instead of diving too much into details, we will simply start creating something with Django and we will learn all the important parts along the way!

Django installation

Virtual environment

Before we install Django we will get you to install an extremely useful tool to help keep your coding environment tidy on your computer. It's possible to skip this step, but it's highly recommended. Starting with the best possible setup will save you a lot of trouble in the future!

So, let's create a **virtual environment** (also called a *virtualenv*). Virtualenv will isolate your Python/Django setup on a per-project basis. This means that any changes you make to one website won't affect any others you're also developing. Neat, right?

All you need to do is find a directory in which you want to create the `virtualenv` ; your home directory, for example. On Windows it might look like `C:\Users\Name\` (where `Name` is the name of your login).

NOTE: On Windows, make sure that this directory does not contain accented or special characters; if your username contains accented characters, use a different directory, for example `c:\djangogirls`.

For this tutorial we will be using a new directory `djangogirls` from your home directory:

command-line

```
$ mkdir djangogirls
$ cd djangogirls
```

We will make a virtualenv called `myvenv` . The general command will be in the format:

command-line

```
$ python3 -m venv myvenv
```

Windows

To create a new `virtualenv` , you need to open the console (we told you about that a few chapters ago – remember?) and run `C:\Python35\python -m venv myvenv` . It will look like this:

command-line

```
C:\Users\Name\djangogirls> C:\Python35\python -m venv myvenv
```

where `C:\Python35\python` is the directory in which you previously installed Python and `myvenv` is the name of your `virtualenv` . You can use any other name, but stick to lowercase and use no spaces, accents or special characters. It is also good idea to keep the name short – you'll be referencing it a lot!

Linux and OS X

Creating a `virtualenv` on both Linux and OS X is as simple as running `python3 -m venv myvenv`. It will look like this:

command-line

```
$ python3 -m venv myvenv
```

`myvenv` is the name of your `virtualenv`. You can use any other name, but stick to lowercase and use no spaces. It is also good idea to keep the name short as you'll be referencing it a lot!

> NOTE: On some versions of Debian/Ubuntu you may receive the following error:
>
> command-line
>
> ```
> The virtual environment was not created successfully because ensurepip is not available.  On Debian/Ubuntu sys
> tems, you need to install the python3-venv package using the following command.
>     apt-get install python3-venv
> You may need to use sudo with that command.  After installing the python3-venv package, recreate your virtual
> environment.
> ```
>
> In this case, follow the instructions above and install the `python3-venv` package:
>
> command-line
>
> ```
> $ sudo apt-get install python3-venv
> ```
>
> NOTE: On some versions of Debian/Ubuntu initiating the virtual environment like this currently gives the following error:
>
> command-line
>
> ```
> Error: Command '['/home/eddie/Slask/tmp/venv/bin/python3', '-Im', 'ensurepip', '--upgrade', '--default-pip']'
> returned non-zero exit status 1
> ```
>
> To get around this, use the `virtualenv` command instead.
>
> command-line
>
> ```
> $ sudo apt-get install python-virtualenv
> $ virtualenv --python=python3.5 myvenv
> ```
>
> NOTE: If you get an error like
>
> command-line
>
> ```
> E: Unable to locate package python3-venv
> ```
>
> then instead run:
>
> command-line
>
> ```
> sudo apt install python3.5-venv
> ```

Working with virtualenv

The command above will create a directory called `myvenv` (or whatever name you chose) that contains our virtual environment (basically a bunch of directory and files).

Windows

Start your virtual environment by running:

command-line

```
C:\Users\Name\djangogirls> myvenv\Scripts\activate
```

NOTE: on Windows 10 you might get an error in the Windows PowerShell that says execution of scripts is disabled on this system. In this case, open another Windows PowerShell with the "Run as Administrator" option. Then try typing the following command before starting your virtual environment:

command-line

```
C:\WINDOWS\system32> Set-ExecutionPolicy -ExecutionPolicy RemoteSigned
    Execution Policy Change
    The execution policy helps protect you from scripts that you do not trust. Changing the execution policy m
ight expose you to the security risks described in the about Execution Policies help topic at http://go.micros
oft.com/fwlink/?LinkID=135170. Do you want to change the execution policy? [Y] Yes  [A] Yes to All  [N] No  [L
] No to All  [S] Suspend  [?] Help (default is "N"): A
```

Linux and OS X

Start your virtual environment by running:

command-line

```
$ source myvenv/bin/activate
```

Remember to replace `myvenv` with your chosen `virtualenv` name!

NOTE: sometimes source might not be available. In those cases try doing this instead:

command-line

```
$ . myvenv/bin/activate
```

You will know that you have `virtualenv` started when you see that the prompt in your console is prefixed with `(myvenv)` .

When working within a virtual environment, `python` will automatically refer to the correct version so you can use `python` instead of `python3` .

OK, we have all important dependencies in place. We can finally install Django!

Installing Django

Now that you have your `virtualenv` started, you can install Django.

Before we do that, we should make sure we have the latest version of `pip` , the software that we use to install Django:

command-line

```
(myvenv) ~$ pip install --upgrade pip
```

Then run `pip install django~=1.10.0` (note that we use a tilde followed by an equal sign: `~=`) to install Django.

command-line

```
(myvenv) ~$ pip install django~=1.10.0
Collecting django~=1.10.0
  Downloading Django-1.10.4-py2.py3-none-any.whl (6.8MB)
Installing collected packages: django
Successfully installed django-1.10.4
```

Windows

If you get an error when calling pip on Windows platform, please check if your project pathname contains spaces, accents or special characters (for example, `C:\Users\User Name\djangogirls`). If it does, please consider using another place without spaces, accents or special characters (suggestion: `C:\djangogirls`). Create a new virtualenv in the new directory, then delete the old one and try the above command again. (Moving the virtualenv directory won't work since virtualenv uses absolute paths.)

Windows 8 and Windows 10

Your command line might freeze after when you try to install Django. If this happens, instead of the above command use:

command-line

```
C:\Users\Name\djangogirls> python -m pip install django~=1.10.0
```

Linux

If you get an error when calling pip on Ubuntu 12.04 please run `python -m pip install -U --force-reinstall pip` to fix the pip installation in the virtualenv.

That's it! You're now (finally) ready to create a Django application!

Your first Django project!

Part of this chapter is based on tutorials by Geek Girls Carrots (https://github.com/ggcarrots/django-carrots).

Parts of this chapter are based on the django-marcador tutorial licensed under the Creative Commons Attribution-ShareAlike 4.0 International License. The django-marcador tutorial is copyrighted by Markus Zapke-Gründemann et al.

We're going to create a simple blog!

The first step is to start a new Django project. Basically, this means that we'll run some scripts provided by Django that will create the skeleton of a Django project for us. This is just a bunch of directories and files that we will use later.

The names of some files and directories are very important for Django. You should not rename the files that we are about to create. Moving them to a different place is also not a good idea. Django needs to maintain a certain structure to be able to find important things.

Remember to run everything in the virtualenv. If you don't see a prefix `(myvenv)` in your console, you need to activate your virtualenv. We explained how to do that in the **Django installation** chapter in the **Working with virtualenv** part. Typing `myvenv\Scripts\activate` on Windows or `source myvenv/bin/activate` on Mac OS X or Linux will do this for you.

OS X or Linux

In your Mac OS X or Linux console, you should run the following command. **Don't forget to add the period (or dot)** `.` **at the end!**

command-line

```
(myvenv) ~/djangogirls$ django-admin startproject mysite .
```

The period `.` is crucial because it tells the script to install Django in your current directory (for which the period `.` is a short-hand reference).

Note When typing the command above, remember that you only type the part which starts by `django-admin`. The `(myvenv) ~/djangogirls$` part shown here is just example of the prompt that will be inviting your input on your command line.

Windows

On Windows you should run the following command. **(Don't forget to add the period (or dot)** `.` **at the end)**:

command-line

```
(myvenv) C:\Users\Name\djangogirls> django-admin.py startproject mysite .
```

The period `.` is crucial because it tells the script to install Django in your current directory (for which the period `.` is a short-hand reference).

Note When typing the command above, remember that you only type the part which starts by `django-admin.py`. The `(myvenv) C:\Users\Name\djangogirls>` part shown here is just example of the prompt that will be inviting your input on your command line.

`django-admin.py` is a script that will create the directories and files for you. You should now have a directory structure which looks like this:

```
djangogirls
├── manage.py
└── mysite
        settings.py
        urls.py
        wsgi.py
        __init__.py
```

> **Note**: in your directory structure, you will also see your `venv` directory that we created before.

`manage.py` is a script that helps with management of the site. With it we will be able (amongst other things) to start a web server on our computer without installing anything else.

The `settings.py` file contains the configuration of your website.

Remember when we talked about a mail carrier checking where to deliver a letter? `urls.py` file contains a list of patterns used by `urlresolver`.

Let's ignore the other files for now as we won't change them. The only thing to remember is not to delete them by accident!

Changing settings

Let's make some changes in `mysite/settings.py`. Open the file using the code editor you installed earlier.

It would be nice to have the correct time on our website. Go to Wikipedia's list of time zones and copy your relevant time zone (TZ) (e.g. `Europe/Berlin`).

In `settings.py`, find the line that contains `TIME_ZONE` and modify it to choose your own timezone. For example:

mysite/settings.py

```
TIME_ZONE = 'Europe/Berlin'
```

We'll also need to add a path for static files. (We'll find out all about static files and CSS later in the tutorial.) Go down to the *end* of the file, and just underneath the `STATIC_URL` entry, add a new one called `STATIC_ROOT`:

mysite/settings.py

```
STATIC_URL = '/static/'
STATIC_ROOT = os.path.join(BASE_DIR, 'static')
```

When `DEBUG` is `True` and `ALLOWED_HOSTS` is empty, the host is validated against `['localhost', '127.0.0.1', '[::1]']`. This won't match our hostname on PythonAnywhere once we deploy our application so we will change the following setting:

mysite/settings.py

```
ALLOWED_HOSTS = ['127.0.0.1', '.pythonanywhere.com']
```

> **Note**: If you're using a Chromebook, add this line at the bottom of your settings.py file: `MESSAGE_STORAGE = 'django.contrib.messages.storage.session.SessionStorage'`

Set up a database

There's a lot of different database software that can store data for your site. We'll use the default one, `sqlite3`.

This is already set up in this part of your `mysite/settings.py` file:

mysite/settings.py

```
DATABASES = {
    'default': {
        'ENGINE': 'django.db.backends.sqlite3',
        'NAME': os.path.join(BASE_DIR, 'db.sqlite3'),
    }
}
```

To create a database for our blog, let's run the following in the console: `python manage.py migrate` (we need to be in the `djangogirls` directory that contains the `manage.py` file). If that goes well, you should see something like this:

command-line

```
(myvenv) ~/djangogirls$ python manage.py migrate
Operations to perform:
  Apply all migrations: auth, admin, contenttypes, sessions
Running migrations:
  Rendering model states... DONE
  Applying contenttypes.0001_initial... OK
  Applying auth.0001_initial... OK
  Applying admin.0001_initial... OK
  Applying admin.0002_logentry_remove_auto_add... OK
  Applying contenttypes.0002_remove_content_type_name... OK
  Applying auth.0002_alter_permission_name_max_length... OK
  Applying auth.0003_alter_user_email_max_length... OK
  Applying auth.0004_alter_user_username_opts... OK
  Applying auth.0005_alter_user_last_login_null... OK
  Applying auth.0006_require_contenttypes_0002... OK
  Applying auth.0007_alter_validators_add_error_messages... OK
  Applying sessions.0001_initial... OK
```

And we're done! Time to start the web server and see if our website is working!

Starting the web server

You need to be in the directory that contains the `manage.py` file (the `djangogirls` directory). In the console, we can start the web server by running `python manage.py runserver` :

command-line

```
(myvenv) ~/djangogirls$ python manage.py runserver
```

If you are on a Chromebook, use this command instead:

Cloud 9

```
(myvenv) ~/djangogirls$ python manage.py runserver 0.0.0.0:8000
```

If you are on Windows and this fails with `UnicodeDecodeError` , use this command instead:

command-line

```
(myvenv) ~/djangogirls$ python manage.py runserver 0:8000
```

Now all you need to do is check that your website is running. Open your browser (Firefox, Chrome, Safari, Internet Explorer or whatever you use) and enter this address:

browser

```
http://127.0.0.1:8000/
```

If you're using a Chromebook, you'll always visit your test server by accessing:

browser

```
https://django-girls-<your cloud9 username>.c9users.io
```

Congratulations! You've just created your first website and run it using a web server! Isn't that awesome?

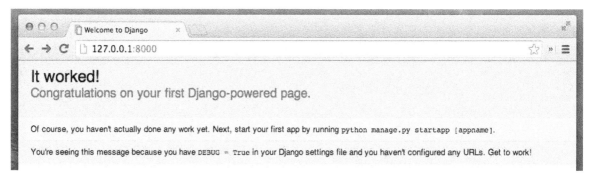

While the web server is running, you won't see a new command-line prompt to enter additional commands. The terminal will accept new text but will not execute new commands. This is because the web server continuously runs in order to listen for incoming requests.

> We reviewed how web servers work in the **How the Internet works** chapter.

To type additional commands while the web server is running, open a new terminal window and activate your virtualenv. To stop the web server, switch back to the window in which it's running and press CTRL+C - Control and C keys together (on Windows, you might have to press Ctrl+Break).

Ready for the next step? It's time to create some content!

Django models

What we want to create now is something that will store all the posts in our blog. But to be able to do that we need to talk a little bit about things called `objects`.

Objects

There is a concept in programming called `object-oriented programming`. The idea is that instead of writing everything as a boring sequence of programming instructions, we can model things and define how they interact with each other.

So what is an object? It is a collection of properties and actions. It sounds weird, but we will give you an example.

If we want to model a cat, we will create an object `Cat` that has some properties such as `color`, `age`, `mood` (like good, bad, or sleepy ;)), and `owner` (which could be assigned a `Person` object – or maybe, in case of a stray cat, this property could be empty).

Then the `Cat` has some actions: `purr`, `scratch`, or `feed` (in which case, we will give the cat some `CatFood`, which could be a separate object with properties, like `taste`).

```
Cat
--------
color
age
mood
owner
purr()
scratch()
feed(cat_food)


CatFood
--------
taste
```

So basically the idea is to describe real things in code with properties (called `object properties`) and actions (called `methods`).

How will we model blog posts then? We want to build a blog, right?

We need to answer the question: What is a blog post? What properties should it have?

Well, for sure our blog post needs some text with its content and a title, right? It would be also nice to know who wrote it – so we need an author. Finally, we want to know when the post was created and published.

```
Post
--------
title
text
author
created_date
published_date
```

What kind of things could be done with a blog post? It would be nice to have some `method` that publishes the post, right?

So we will need a `publish` method.

Since we already know what we want to achieve, let's start modeling it in Django!

Django model

Knowing what an object is, we can create a Django model for our blog post.

A model in Django is a special kind of object – it is saved in the `database`. A database is a collection of data. This is a place in which you will store information about users, your blog posts, etc. We will be using a SQLite database to store our data. This is the default Django database adapter – it'll be enough for us right now.

You can think of a model in the database as a spreadsheet with columns (fields) and rows (data).

Creating an application

To keep everything tidy, we will create a separate application inside our project. It is very nice to have everything organized from the very beginning. To create an application we need to run the following command in the console (from `djangogirls` directory where `manage.py` file is):

command-line

```
(myvenv) ~/djangogirls$ python manage.py startapp blog
```

You will notice that a new `blog` directory is created and it contains a number of files now. The directories and files in our project should look like this:

```
djangogirls
├── blog
│   ├── __init__.py
│   ├── admin.py
│   ├── apps.py
│   ├── migrations
│   │   └── __init__.py
│   ├── models.py
│   ├── tests.py
│   └── views.py
├── db.sqlite3
├── manage.py
└── mysite
    ├── __init__.py
    ├── settings.py
    ├── urls.py
    └── wsgi.py
```

After creating an application, we also need to tell Django that it should use it. We do that in the file `mysite/settings.py`. We need to find `INSTALLED_APPS` and add a line containing `'blog',` just above `]`. So the final product should look like this:

mysite/settings.py

```
INSTALLED_APPS = [
    'django.contrib.admin',
    'django.contrib.auth',
    'django.contrib.contenttypes',
    'django.contrib.sessions',
    'django.contrib.messages',
    'django.contrib.staticfiles',
    'blog',
]
```

Creating a blog post model

In the `blog/models.py` file we define all objects called `Models` – this is a place in which we will define our blog post.

Let's open `blog/models.py`, remove everything from it, and write code like this:

blog/models.py

```
from django.db import models
from django.utils import timezone


class Post(models.Model):
    author = models.ForeignKey('auth.User')
    title = models.CharField(max_length=200)
    text = models.TextField()
    created_date = models.DateTimeField(
            default=timezone.now)
    published_date = models.DateTimeField(
            blank=True, null=True)

    def publish(self):
        self.published_date = timezone.now()
        self.save()

    def __str__(self):
        return self.title
```

Double-check that you use two underscore characters (_) on each side of `str`. This convention is used frequently in Python and sometimes we also call them "dunder" (short for "double-underscore").

It looks scary, right? But don't worry – we will explain what these lines mean!

All lines starting with `from` or `import` are lines that add some bits from other files. So instead of copying and pasting the same things in every file, we can include some parts with `from ... import ... .`

`class Post(models.Model):` – this line defines our model (it is an `object`).

- `class` is a special keyword that indicates that we are defining an object.
- `Post` is the name of our model. We can give it a different name (but we must avoid special characters and whitespace). Always start a class name with an uppercase letter.
- `models.Model` means that the Post is a Django Model, so Django knows that it should be saved in the database.

Now we define the properties we were talking about: `title` , `text` , `created_date` , `published_date` and `author` . To do that we need to define the type of each field (Is it text? A number? A date? A relation to another object, like a User?)

- `models.CharField` – this is how you define text with a limited number of characters.
- `models.TextField` – this is for long text without a limit. Sounds ideal for blog post content, right?
- `models.DateTimeField` – this is a date and time.
- `models.ForeignKey` – this is a link to another model.

We will not explain every bit of code here since it would take too much time. You should take a look at Django's documentation if you want to know more about Model fields and how to define things other than those described above (https://docs.djangoproject.com/en/1.10/ref/models/fields/#field-types).

What about `def publish(self):` ? This is exactly the `publish` method we were talking about before. `def` means that this is a function/method and `publish` is the name of the method. You can change the name of the method if you want. The naming rule is that we use lowercase and underscores instead of spaces. For example, a method that calculates average price could be called `calculate_average_price` .

Methods often `return` something. There is an example of that in the `__str__` method. In this scenario, when we call `__str__()` we will get a text (**string**) with a Post title.

Also notice that both `def publish(self):` and `def __str__(self):` are indented inside our class. Because Python is sensitive to whitespace, we need to indent our methods inside the class. Otherwise, the methods won't belong to the class, and you can get some unexpected behavior.

If something is still not clear about models, feel free to ask your coach! We know it is complicated, especially when you learn what objects and functions are at the same time. But hopefully it looks slightly less magic for you now!

Create tables for models in your database

The last step here is to add our new model to our database. First we have to make Django know that we have some changes in our model. (We have just created it!) Go to your console window and type `python manage.py makemigrations blog`. It will look like this:

command-line

```
(myvenv) ~/djangogirls$ python manage.py makemigrations blog
Migrations for 'blog':
  blog/migrations/0001_initial.py:
  - Create model Post
```

Note: Remember to save the files you edit. Otherwise, your computer will execute the previous version which might give you unexpected error messages.

Django prepared a migration file for us that we now have to apply to our database. Type `python manage.py migrate blog` and the output should be as follows:

command-line

```
(myvenv) ~/djangogirls$ python manage.py migrate blog
Operations to perform:
  Apply all migrations: blog
Running migrations:
  Rendering model states... DONE
  Applying blog.0001_initial... OK
```

Hurray! Our Post model is now in our database! It would be nice to see it, right? Jump to the next chapter to see what your Post looks like!

Django admin

To add, edit and delete the posts we've just modeled, we will use Django admin.

Let's open the `blog/admin.py` file and replace its contents with this:

blog/admin.py

```
from django.contrib import admin
from .models import Post

admin.site.register(Post)
```

As you can see, we import (include) the Post model defined in the previous chapter. To make our model visible on the admin page, we need to register the model with `admin.site.register(Post)`.

OK, time to look at our Post model. Remember to run `python manage.py runserver` in the console to run the web server. Go to your browser and type the address http://127.0.0.1:8000/admin/. You will see a login page like this:

Django administration

Username:

Password:

Log in

To log in, you need to create a *superuser* - a user account that has control over everything on the site. Go back to the command line, type `python manage.py createsuperuser`, and press enter.

Remember, to write new commands while the web server is running, open a new terminal window and activate your virtualenv. We reviewed how to write new commands in the **Your first Django project!** chapter, in the **Starting the web server** section.

When prompted, type your username (lowercase, no spaces), email address, and password. Don't worry that you can't see the password you're typing in – that's how it's supposed to be. Just type it in and press `enter` to continue. The output should look like this (where the username and email should be your own ones):

command-line

```
(myvenv) ~/djangogirls$ python manage.py createsuperuser
Username: admin
Email address: admin@admin.com
Password:
Password (again):
Superuser created successfully.
```

Return to your browser. Log in with the superuser's credentials you chose; you should see the Django admin dashboard.

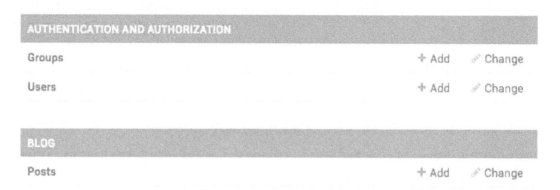

Go to Posts and experiment a little bit with it. Add five or six blog posts. Don't worry about the content – you can simply copy-paste some text from this tutorial to save time. :)

Make sure that at least two or three posts (but not all) have the publish date set. It will be helpful later.

If you want to know more about Django admin, you should check Django's documentation:
https://docs.djangoproject.com/en/1.10/ref/contrib/admin/

This is probably a good moment to grab a coffee (or tea) or something to eat to re-energize yourself. You created your first Django model – you deserve a little break!

Deploy!

> Note The following chapter can be sometimes a bit hard to get through. Persist and finish it; deployment is an important part of the website development process. This chapter is placed in the middle of the tutorial so that your mentor can help with the slightly trickier process of getting your website online. This means you can still finish the tutorial on your own if you run out of time

Until now, your website was only available on your computer. Now you will learn how to deploy it! Deploying is the process of publishing your application on the Internet so people can finally go and see your app. :)

As you learned, a website has to be located on a server. There are a lot of server providers available on the internet. We will use one that has a relatively simple deployment process: PythonAnywhere. PythonAnywhere is free for small applications that don't have too many visitors so it'll definitely be enough for you now.

The other external service we'll be using is GitHub, which is a code hosting service. There are others out there, but almost all programmers have a GitHub account these days, and now so will you!

These three places will be important to you. Your local computer will be the place where you do development and testing. When you're happy with the changes, you will place a copy of your program on GitHub. Your website will be on PythonAnywhere and you will update it by getting a new copy of your code from GitHub.

Git

> Note If you already did the Installation steps, there's no need to do this again -- you can skip to the next section and start creating your Git repository

Git is a "version control system" used by a lot of programmers. This software can track changes to files over time so that you can recall specific versions later. A bit like the "track changes" feature in Microsoft Word, but much more powerful.

Installing Git

Windows

You can download Git from git-scm.com. You can hit "next" on all steps except for one; in the fifth step entitled "Adjusting your PATH environment", choose "Use Git and optional Unix tools from the Windows Command Prompt" (the bottom option). Other than that, the defaults are fine. Checkout Windows-style, commit Unix-style line endings is good.

OS X

Download Git from git-scm.com and just follow the instructions.

> Note If you are running OS X 10.6, 10.7, or 10.8, you will need to install the version of git from here. Git installer for OS X Snow Leopard

Debian or Ubuntu

command-line

```
$ sudo apt-get install git
```

Fedora (up to 21)

command-line

```
$ sudo yum install git
```

Fedora 22+

command-line

```
$ sudo dnf install git
```

openSUSE

command-line

```
$ sudo zypper install git
```

Starting our Git repository

Git tracks changes to a particular set of files in what's called a code repository (or "repo" for short). Let's start one for our project. Open up your console and run these commands, in the `djangogirls` directory:

> Note Check your current working directory with a `pwd` (Mac OS X/Linux) or `cd` (Windows) command before initializing the repository. You should be in the `djangogirls` folder.

command-line

```
$ git init
Initialized empty Git repository in ~/djangogirls/.git/
$ git config --global user.name "Your Name"
$ git config --global user.email you@example.com
```

Initializing the git repository is something we need to do only once per project (and you won't have to re-enter the username and email ever again).

Git will track changes to all the files and folders in this directory, but there are some files we want it to ignore. We do this by creating a file called `.gitignore` in the base directory. Open up your editor and create a new file with the following contents:

.gitignore

```
*.pyc
*~
__pycache__
myvenv
db.sqlite3
/static
.DS_Store
```

And save it as `.gitignore` in the "djangogirls" folder.

It's a good idea to use a `git status` command before `git add` or whenever you find yourself unsure of what has changed. This will help prevent any surprises from happening, such as wrong files being added or committed. The `git status` command returns information about any untracked/modified/staged files, the branch status, and much more. The output should be similar to the following:

command-line

```
$ git status
On branch master

Initial commit

Untracked files:
  (use "git add <file>..." to include in what will be committed)

        .gitignore
        blog/
        manage.py
        mysite/

nothing added to commit but untracked files present (use "git add" to track)
```

And finally we save our changes. Go to your console and run these commands:

command-line

```
$ git add --all .
$ git commit -m "My Django Girls app, first commit"
 [...]
 13 files changed, 200 insertions(+)
 create mode 100644 .gitignore
 [...]
 create mode 100644 mysite/wsgi.py
```

Pushing your code to GitHub

Go to GitHub.com and sign up for a new, free user account. (If you already did that in the workshop prep, that is great!)

Then, create a new repository, giving it the name "my-first-blog". Leave the "initialize with a README" checkbox unchecked, leave the .gitignore option blank (we've done that manually) and leave the License as None.

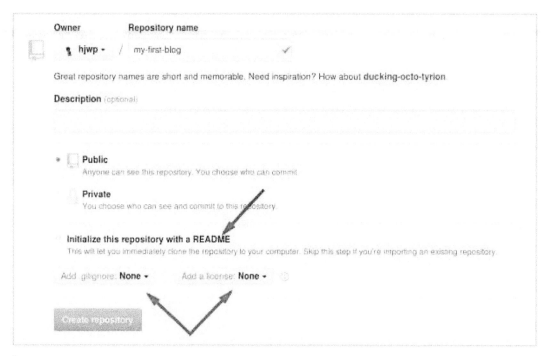

Note The name `my-first-blog` is important – you could choose something else, but it's going to occur lots of times in the instructions below, and you'd have to substitute it each time. It's probably easier to just stick with the name `my-first-blog`.

On the next screen, you'll be shown your repo's clone URL. Choose the "HTTPS" version, copy it, and we'll paste it into the terminal shortly:

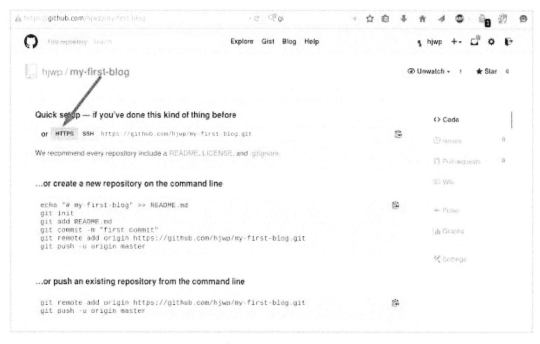

Now we need to hook up the Git repository on your computer to the one up on GitHub.

Type the following into your console (Replace `<your-github-username>` with the username you entered when you created your GitHub account, but without the angle-brackets):

command-line

```
$ git remote add origin https://github.com/<your-github-username>/my-first-blog.git
$ git push -u origin master
```

Enter your GitHub username and password and you should see something like this:

command-line

```
Username for 'https://github.com': hjwp
Password for 'https://hjwp@github.com':
Counting objects: 6, done.
Writing objects: 100% (6/6), 200 bytes | 0 bytes/s, done.
Total 3 (delta 0), reused 0 (delta 0)
To https://github.com/hjwp/my-first-blog.git
 * [new branch]      master -> master
Branch master set up to track remote branch master from origin.
```

Your code is now on GitHub. Go and check it out! You'll find it's in fine company – Django, the Django Girls Tutorial, and many other great open source software projects also host their code on GitHub. :)

Setting up our blog on PythonAnywhere

> Note You might have already created a PythonAnywhere account earlier during the install steps – if so, no need to do it again.

Next it's time to sign up for a free "Beginner" account on PythonAnywhere.

- www.pythonanywhere.com

> Note When choosing your username here, bear in mind that your blog's URL will take the form yourusername.pythonanywhere.com , so choose either your own nickname, or a name for what your blog is all about.

Pulling our code down on PythonAnywhere

When you've signed up for PythonAnywhere, you'll be taken to your dashboard or "Consoles" page. Choose the option to start a "Bash" console – that's the PythonAnywhere version of a console, just like the one on your computer.

> Note PythonAnywhere is based on Linux, so if you're on Windows, the console will look a little different from the one on your computer.

Let's pull down our code from GitHub and onto PythonAnywhere by creating a "clone" of our repo. Type the following into the console on PythonAnywhere (don't forget to use your GitHub username in place of `<your-github-username>`):

PythonAnywhere command-line

```
$ git clone https://github.com/<your-github-username>/my-first-blog.git
```

This will pull down a copy of your code onto PythonAnywhere. Check it out by typing `tree my-first-blog` :

PythonAnywhere command-line

```
$ tree my-first-blog
my-first-blog/
├── blog
│   ├── __init__.py
│   ├── admin.py
│   ├── migrations
│   │   ├── 0001_initial.py
│   │   └── __init__.py
│   ├── models.py
│   ├── tests.py
│   └── views.py
├── manage.py
└── mysite
    ├── __init__.py
    ├── settings.py
    ├── urls.py
    └── wsgi.py
```

Creating a virtualenv on PythonAnywhere

Just like you did on your own computer, you can create a virtualenv on PythonAnywhere. In the Bash console, type:

PythonAnywhere command-line

```
$ cd my-first-blog

$ virtualenv --python=python3.5 myvenv
Running virtualenv with interpreter /usr/bin/python3.5
[...]
Installing setuptools, pip...done.

$ source myvenv/bin/activate

(myvenv) $  pip install django~=1.10.0
Collecting django
[...]
Successfully installed django-1.10.4
```

> Note The `pip install` step can take a couple of minutes. Patience, patience! But if it takes more than five minutes, something is wrong. Ask your coach.

Creating the database on PythonAnywhere

Here's another thing that's different between your own computer and the server: it uses a different database. So the user accounts and posts can be different on the server and on your computer.

We can initialize the database on the server just like we did the one on your own computer, with `migrate` and `createsuperuser`:

PythonAnywhere command-line

```
(mvenv) $ python manage.py migrate
Operations to perform:
[...]
  Applying sessions.0001_initial... OK
(mvenv) $ python manage.py createsuperuser
```

Publishing our blog as a web app

Now our code is on PythonAnywhere, our virtualenv is ready, and the database is initialized. We're ready to publish it as a web app!

Click back to the PythonAnywhere dashboard by clicking on its logo, and then click on the **Web** tab. Finally, hit **Add a new web app**.

After confirming your domain name, choose **manual configuration** (N.B. – *not* the "Django" option) in the dialog. Next choose **Python 3.5**, and click Next to finish the wizard.

> Note Make sure you choose the "Manual configuration" option, not the "Django" one. We're too cool for the default PythonAnywhere Django setup. :-)

Setting the virtualenv

You'll be taken to the PythonAnywhere config screen for your webapp, which is where you'll need to go whenever you want to make changes to the app on the server.

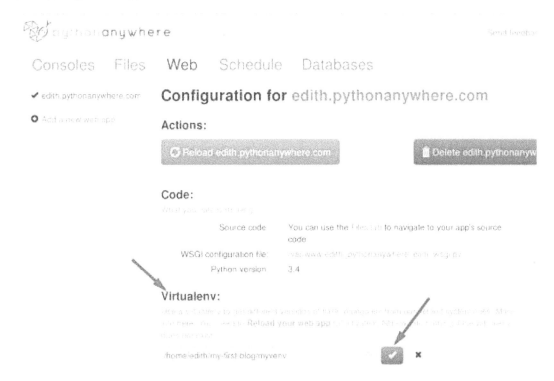

In the "Virtualenv" section, click the red text that says "Enter the path to a virtualenv", and enter `/home/<your-PythonAnywhere-username>/my-first-blog/myvenv/` . Click the blue box with the checkmark to save the path before moving on.

> Note Substitute your own PythonAnywhere username as appropriate. If you make a mistake, PythonAnywhere will show you a little warning.

Configuring the WSGI file

Django works using the "WSGI protocol", a standard for serving websites using Python, which PythonAnywhere supports. The way we configure PythonAnywhere to recognize our Django blog is by editing a WSGI configuration file.

Click on the "WSGI configuration file" link (in the "Code" section near the top of the page – it'll be named something like `/var/www/<your-PythonAnywhere-username>_pythonanywhere_com_wsgi.py`), and you'll be taken to an editor.

Delete all the contents and replace them with something like this:

<your-username>_pythonanywhere_com_wsgi.py

```
import os
import sys

path = '/home/<your-PythonAnywhere-username>/my-first-blog'  # use your own PythonAnywhere username here
if path not in sys.path:
    sys.path.append(path)

os.environ['DJANGO_SETTINGS_MODULE'] = 'mysite.settings'

from django.core.wsgi import get_wsgi_application
from django.contrib.staticfiles.handlers import StaticFilesHandler
application = StaticFilesHandler(get_wsgi_application())
```

> **Note** Don't forget to substitute in your own PythonAnywhere username where it says `<your-PythonAnywhere-username>`. **Note** In line four, we make sure Python anywhere knows how to find our application. It is very important that this path name is correct, and especially that there are no extra spaces here. Otherwise you will see an "ImportError" in the error log.

This file's job is to tell PythonAnywhere where our web app lives and what the Django settings file's name is.

The `StaticFilesHandler` is for dealing with our CSS. This is taken care of automatically for you during local development by the `runserver` command. We'll find out a bit more about static files later in the tutorial, when we edit the CSS for our site.

Hit **Save** and then go back to the **Web** tab.

We're all done! Hit the big green **Reload** button and you'll be able to go view your application. You'll find a link to it at the top of the page.

Debugging tips

If you see an error when you try to visit your site, the first place to look for some debugging info is in your **error log**. You'll find a link to this on the PythonAnywhere Web tab. See if there are any error messages in there; the most recent ones are at the bottom. Common problems include:

- Forgetting one of the steps we did in the console: creating the virtualenv, activating it, installing Django into it, migrating the database.

- Making a mistake in the virtualenv path on the Web tab – there will usually be a little red error message on there, if there is a problem.

- Making a mistake in the WSGI configuration file – did you get the path to your my-first-blog folder right?

- Did you pick the same version of Python for your virtualenv as you did for your web app? Both should be 3.5.

There are also some general debugging tips on the PythonAnywhere wiki.

And remember, your coach is here to help!

You are live!

The default page for your site should say "It worked!", just like it does on your local computer. Try adding `/admin/` to the end of the URL, and you'll be taken to the admin site. Log in with the username and password, and you'll see you can add new Posts on the server.

Once you have a few posts created, you can go back to your local setup (not PythonAnywhere). From here you should work on your local setup to make changes. This is a common workflow in web development – make changes locally, push those changes to GitHub, and pull your changes down to your live Web server. This allows you to work and experiment without breaking your live Web site. Pretty cool, huh?

Give yourself a *HUGE* pat on the back! Server deployments are one of the trickiest parts of web development and it often takes people several days before they get them working. But you've got your site live, on the real Internet, just like that!

Django URLs

We're about to build our first webpage: a homepage for your blog! But first, let's learn a little bit about Django URLs.

What is a URL?

A URL is simply a web address. You can see a URL every time you visit a website – it is visible in your browser's address bar. (Yes! `127.0.0.1:8000` is a URL! And `https://djangogirls.org` is also a URL.)

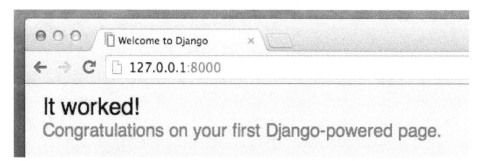

Every page on the Internet needs its own URL. This way your application knows what it should show to a user who opens that URL. In Django we use something called `URLconf` (URL configuration). URLconf is a set of patterns that Django will try to match with the requested URL to find the correct view.

How do URLs work in Django?

Let's open up the `mysite/urls.py` file in your code editor of choice and see what it looks like:

mysite/urls.py

```
"""mysite URL Configuration

[...]
"""
from django.conf.urls import url
from django.contrib import admin

urlpatterns = [
    url(r'^admin/', admin.site.urls),
]
```

As you can see, Django has already put something here for us.

Lines between triple quotes (`'''` or `"""`) are called docstrings – you can write them at the top of a file, class or method to describe what it does. They won't be run by Python.

The admin URL, which you visited in previous chapter, is already here:

mysite/urls.py

```
    url(r'^admin/', admin.site.urls),
```

This line means that for every URL that starts with `admin/` , Django will find a corresponding *view*. In this case we're including a lot of admin URLs so it isn't all packed into this small file – it's more readable and cleaner.

Regex

Do you wonder how Django matches URLs to views? Well, this part is tricky. Django uses `regex`, short for "regular expressions". Regex has a lot (a lot!) of rules that form a search pattern. Since regexes are an advanced topic, we will not go in detail over how they work.

If you still wish to understand how we created the patterns, here is an example of the process – we will only need a limited subset of the rules to express the pattern we are looking for, namely:

- `^` for the beginning of the text
- `$` for the end of the text
- `\d` for a digit
- `+` to indicate that the previous item should be repeated at least once
- `()` to capture part of the pattern

Anything else in the URL definition will be taken literally.

Now imagine you have a website with the address like `http://www.mysite.com/post/12345/`, where `12345` is the number of your post.

Writing separate views for all the post numbers would be really annoying. With regular expressions, we can create a pattern that will match the URL and extract the number for us: `^post/(\d+)/$`. Let's break this down piece by piece to see what we are doing here:

- **^post/** is telling Django to take anything that has `post/` at the beginning of the url (right after `^`)
- **(\d+)** means that there will be a number (one or more digits) and that we want the number captured and extracted
- **/** tells django that another `/` character should follow
- **$** then indicates the end of the URL meaning that only strings ending with the `/` will match this pattern

Your first Django URL!

Time to create our first URL! We want 'http://127.0.0.1:8000/' to be the home page of our blog and to display a list of posts.

We also want to keep the `mysite/urls.py` file clean, so we will import URLs from our `blog` application to the main `mysite/urls.py` file.

Go ahead, add a line that will import `blog.urls`. Note that we are using the `include` function here so **you will need** to add that to the import on the first line of the file.

Your `mysite/urls.py` file should now look like this:

mysite/urls.py

```
from django.conf.urls import include, url
from django.contrib import admin

urlpatterns = [
    url(r'^admin/', admin.site.urls),
    url(r'', include('blog.urls')),
]
```

Django will now redirect everything that comes into 'http://127.0.0.1:8000/' to `blog.urls` and look for further instructions there.

Writing regular expressions in Python is always done with `r` in front of the string. This is a helpful hint for Python that the string may contain special characters that are not meant for Python itself, but for the regular expression instead.

blog.urls

Create a new empty file named `blog/urls.py` . All right! Add these first two lines:

blog/urls.py

```
from django.conf.urls import url
from . import views
```

Here we're importing Django's function `url` and all of our `views` from the `blog` application. (We don't have any yet, but we will get to that in a minute!)

After that, we can add our first URL pattern:

blog/urls.py

```
urlpatterns = [
    url(r'^$', views.post_list, name='post_list'),
]
```

As you can see, we're now assigning a `view` called `post_list` to the `^$` URL. This regular expression will match `^` (a beginning) followed by `$` (an end) – so only an empty string will match. That's correct, because in Django URL resolvers, 'http://127.0.0.1:8000/' is not a part of the URL. This pattern will tell Django that `views.post_list` is the right place to go if someone enters your website at the 'http://127.0.0.1:8000/' address.

The last part, `name='post_list'` , is the name of the URL that will be used to identify the view. This can be the same as the name of the view but it can also be something completely different. We will be using the named URLs later in the project, so it is important to name each URL in the app. We should also try to keep the names of URLs unique and easy to remember.

If you try to visit http://127.0.0.1:8000/ now, then you'll find some sort of 'web page not available' message. This is because the server (remember typing `runserver` ?) is no longer running. Take a look at your server console window to find out why.

```
    return _bootstrap._gcd_import(name[level:], package, level)
  File "<frozen importlib._bootstrap>", line 2254, in _gcd_import
  File "<frozen importlib._bootstrap>", line 2237, in _find_and_load
  File "<frozen importlib._bootstrap>", line 2226, in _find_and_load_unlocked
  File "<frozen importlib._bootstrap>", line 1200, in _load_unlocked
  File "<frozen importlib._bootstrap>", line 1129, in _exec
  File "<frozen importlib._bootstrap>", line 1471, in exec_module
  File "<frozen importlib._bootstrap>", line 321, in _call_with_frames_removed
  File "/Users/dana/Dana-Files/Codes/djangogirls/blog/urls.py", line 5, in <module>
    url(r'^$', views.post_list, name='post_list'),
AttributeError: 'module' object has no attribute 'post_list'
```

Your console is showing an error, but don't worry – it's actually pretty useful: It's telling you that there is **no attribute 'post_list'**. That's the name of the *view* that Django is trying to find and use, but we haven't created it yet. At this stage your `/admin/` will also not work. No worries – we will get there.

> If you want to know more about Django URLconfs, look at the official documentation:
> https://docs.djangoproject.com/en/1.10/topics/http/urls/

Django views – time to create!

Time to get rid of the bug we created in the last chapter! :)

A *view* is a place where we put the "logic" of our application. It will request information from the `model` you created before and pass it to a `template`. We'll create a template in the next chapter. Views are just Python functions that are a little bit more complicated than the ones we wrote in the **Introduction to Python** chapter.

Views are placed in the `views.py` file. We will add our *views* to the `blog/views.py` file.

blog/views.py

OK, let's open up this file and see what's in there:

blog/views.py

```
from django.shortcuts import render

# Create your views here.
```

Not too much stuff here yet.

Remember that lines starting with `#` are comments – this means that those lines won't be run by Python.

The simplest *view* can look like this:

blog/views.py

```
def post_list(request):
    return render(request, 'blog/post_list.html', {})
```

As you can see, we created a function (`def`) called `post_list` that takes `request` and `return` a function `render` that will render (put together) our template `blog/post_list.html` .

Save the file, go to http://127.0.0.1:8000/ and see what we've got.

Another error! Read what's going on now:

This shows that the server is running again, at least, but it still doesn't look right, does it? Don't worry, it's just an error page, nothing to be scared of! Just like the error messages in the console, these are actually pretty useful. You can read that the *TemplateDoesNotExist*. Let's fix this bug and create a template in the next chapter!

Learn more about Django views by reading the official documentation:
https://docs.djangoproject.com/en/1.10/topics/http/views/

Django views – time to create!

Introduction to HTML

What's a template, you may ask?

A template is a file that we can re-use to present different information in a consistent format – for example, you could use a template to help you write a letter, because although each letter might contain a different message and be addressed to a different person, they will share the same format.

A Django template's format is described in a language called HTML (that's the HTML we mentioned in the first chapter, **How the Internet works**).

What is HTML?

HTML is a simple code that is interpreted by your web browser – such as Chrome, Firefox or Safari – to display a web page for the user.

HTML stands for "HyperText Markup Language". **HyperText** means it's a type of text that supports hyperlinks between pages. **Markup** means we have taken a document and marked it up with code to tell something (in this case, a browser) how to interpret the page. HTML code is built with **tags**, each one starting with < and ending with > . These tags represent markup **elements**.

Your first template!

Creating a template means creating a template file. Everything is a file, right? You have probably noticed this already.

Templates are saved in `blog/templates/blog` directory. So first create a directory called `templates` inside your blog directory. Then create another directory called `blog` inside your templates directory:

```
blog
└──templates
    └──blog
```

(You might wonder why we need two directories both called `blog` – as you will discover later, this is simply a useful naming convention that makes life easier when things start to get more complicated.)

And now create a `post_list.html` file (just leave it blank for now) inside the `blog/templates/blog` directory.

See how your website looks now: http://127.0.0.1:8000/

> If you still have an error `TemplateDoesNotExist` , try to restart your server. Go into command line, stop the server by pressing Ctrl+C (Control and C keys together) and start it again by running a `python manage.py runserver` command.

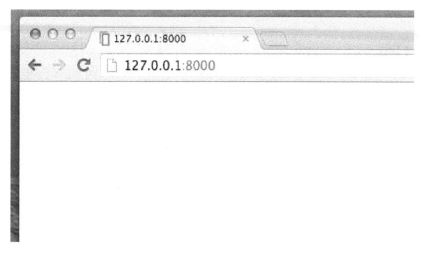

No error anymore! Congratulations :) However, your website isn't actually publishing anything except an empty page, because your template is empty too. We need to fix that.

Add the following to your template file:

blog/templates/blog/post_list.html

```
<html>
    <p>Hi there!</p>
    <p>It works!</p>
</html>
```

So how does your website look now? Visit it to find out: http://127.0.0.1:8000/

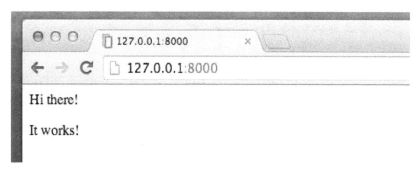

It worked! Nice work there :)

- The most basic tag, `<html>` , is always the beginning of any web page and `</html>` is always the end. As you can see, the whole content of the website goes between the beginning tag `<html>` and closing tag `</html>`
- `<p>` is a tag for paragraph elements; `</p>` closes each paragraph

Head and body

Each HTML page is also divided into two elements: **head** and **body**.

- **head** is an element that contains information about the document that is not displayed on the screen.
- **body** is an element that contains everything else that is displayed as part of the web page.

We use `<head>` to tell the browser about the configuration of the page, and `<body>` to tell it what's actually on the page.

For example, you can put a web page title element inside the `<head>` , like this:

blog/templates/blog/post_list.html

```
<html>
    <head>
        <title>Ola's blog</title>
    </head>
    <body>
        <p>Hi there!</p>
        <p>It works!</p>
    </body>
</html>
```

Save the file and refresh your page.

Notice how the browser has understood that "Ola's blog" is the title of your page? It has interpreted `<title>Ola's blog</title>` and placed the text in the title bar of your browser (it will also be used for bookmarks and so on).

Probably you have also noticed that each opening tag is matched by a *closing tag*, with a `/`, and that elements are *nested* (i.e. you can't close a particular tag until all the ones that were inside it have been closed too).

It's like putting things into boxes. You have one big box, `<html></html>`; inside it there is `<body></body>`, and that contains still smaller boxes: `<p></p>`.

You need to follow these rules of *closing* tags, and of *nesting* elements – if you don't, the browser may not be able to interpret them properly and your page will display incorrectly.

Customize your template

You can now have a little fun and try to customize your template! Here are a few useful tags for that:

- `<h1>A heading</h1>` for your most important heading
- `<h2>A sub-heading</h2>` for a heading at the next level
- `<h3>A sub-sub-heading</h3>` ...and so on, up to `<h6>`
- `<p>A paragraph of text</p>`
- `<em>text</em>` emphasizes your text
- `<strong>text</strong>` strongly emphasizes your text
- `<br />` goes to another line (you can't put anything inside br)
- `<a href="https://djangogirls.org">link</a>` creates a link
- `<ul><li>first item</li><li>second item</li></ul>` makes a list, just like this one!
- `<div></div>` defines a section of the page

Here's an example of a full template, copy and paste it into `blog/templates/blog/post_list.html`:

blog/templates/blog/post_list.html

```
<html>
    <head>
        <title>Django Girls blog</title>
    </head>
    <body>
        <div>
            <h1><a href="">Django Girls Blog</a></h1>
        </div>

        <div>
            <p>published: 14.06.2014, 12:14</p>
            <h2><a href="">My first post</a></h2>
            <p>Aenean eu leo quam. Pellentesque ornare sem lacinia quam venenatis vestibulum. Donec id elit non mi po
rta gravida at eget metus. Fusce dapibus, tellus ac cursus commodo, tortor mauris condimentum nibh, ut fermentum mass
a justo sit amet risus.</p>
        </div>

        <div>
            <p>published: 14.06.2014, 12:14</p>
            <h2><a href="">My second post</a></h2>
            <p>Aenean eu leo quam. Pellentesque ornare sem lacinia quam venenatis vestibulum. Donec id elit non mi po
rta gravida at eget metus. Fusce dapibus, tellus ac cursus commodo, tortor mauris condimentum nibh, ut f.</p>
        </div>
    </body>
</html>
```

We've created three `div` sections here.

- The first `div` element contains the title of our blog – it's a heading and a link
- Another two `div` elements contain our blogposts with a published date, `h2` with a post title that is clickable and two `p` s (paragraph) of text, one for the date and one for our blogpost.

It gives us this effect:

Yaaay! But so far, our template only ever displays exactly **the same information** – whereas earlier we were talking about templates as allowing us to display **different** information in the **same format**.

What we really want to do is display real posts added in our Django admin – and that's where we're going next.

One more thing: deploy!

It'd be good to see all this out and live on the Internet, right? Let's do another PythonAnywhere deploy:

Commit, and push your code up to Github

First off, let's see what files have changed since we last deployed (run these commands locally, not on PythonAnywhere):

command-line

```
$ git status
```

Make sure you're in the `djangogirls` directory and let's tell `git` to include all the changes within this directory:

command-line

```
$ git add --all .
```

> `--all` means that `git` will also recognize if you've deleted files (by default, it only recognizes new/modified files). Also remember (from chapter 3) that `.` means the current directory.

Before we upload all the files, let's check what `git` will be uploading (all the files that `git` will upload should now appear in green):

command-line

```
$ git status
```

We're almost there, now it's time to tell it to save this change in its history. We're going to give it a "commit message" where we describe what we've changed. You can type anything you'd like at this stage, but it's helpful to type something descriptive so that you can remember what you've done in the future.

command-line

```
$ git commit -m "Changed the HTML for the site."
```

> Make sure you use double quotes around the commit message.

Once we've done that, we upload (push) our changes up to GitHub:

command-line

```
$ git push
```

Pull your new code down to PythonAnywhere, and reload your web app

- Open up the PythonAnywhere consoles page and go to your **Bash console** (or start a new one). Then, run:

command-line

```
$ cd ~/my-first-blog
$ git pull
[...]
```

And watch your code get downloaded. If you want to check that it's arrived, you can hop over to the **Files tab** and view your code on PythonAnywhere.

- Finally, hop on over to the Web tab and hit **Reload** on your web app.

Your update should be live! Go ahead and refresh your website in the browser. Changes should be visible. :)

Django ORM and QuerySets

In this chapter you'll learn how Django connects to the database and stores data in it. Let's dive in!

What is a QuerySet?

A QuerySet is, in essence, a list of objects of a given Model. QuerySets allow you to read the data from the database, filter it and order it.

It's easiest to learn by example. Let's try this, shall we?

Django shell

Open up your local console (not on PythonAnywhere) and type this command:

command-line

```
(myvenv) ~/djangogirls$ python manage.py shell
```

The effect should be like this:

command-line

```
(InteractiveConsole)
>>>
```

You're now in Django's interactive console. It's just like the Python prompt, but with some additional Django magic. :) You can use all the Python commands here too, of course.

All objects

Let's try to display all of our posts first. You can do that with the following command:

command-line

```
>>> Post.objects.all()
Traceback (most recent call last):
      File "<console>", line 1, in <module>
NameError: name 'Post' is not defined
```

Oops! An error showed up. It tells us that there is no Post. It's correct – we forgot to import it first!

command-line

```
>>> from blog.models import Post
```

This is simple: we import the model `Post` from `blog.models` . Let's try displaying all posts again:

command-line

```
>>> Post.objects.all()
<QuerySet [<Post: my post title>, <Post: another post title>]>
```

This is a list of the posts we created earlier! We created these posts using the Django admin interface. But now we want to create new posts using Python, so how do we do that?

Create object

This is how you create a new Post object in database:

command-line

```
>>> Post.objects.create(author=me, title='Sample title', text='Test')
```

But we have one missing ingredient here: `me` . We need to pass an instance of `User` model as an author. How do we do that?

Let's import User model first:

command-line

```
>>> from django.contrib.auth.models import User
```

What users do we have in our database? Try this:

command-line

```
>>> User.objects.all()
<QuerySet [<User: ola>]>
```

This is the superuser we created earlier! Let's get an instance of the user now:

command-line

```
>>> me = User.objects.get(username='ola')
```

As you can see, we now `get` a `User` with a `username` that equals 'ola'. Neat! Of course, you have to adjust this line to use your own username.

Now we can finally create our post:

command-line

```
>>> Post.objects.create(author=me, title='Sample title', text='Test')
```

Hurray! Wanna check if it worked?

command-line

```
>>> Post.objects.all()
<QuerySet [<Post: my post title>, <Post: another post title>, <Post: Sample title>]>
```

There it is, one more post in the list!

Add more posts

You can now have a little fun and add more posts to see how it works. Add two or three more and then go ahead to the next part.

Filter objects

A big part of QuerySets is the ability to filter them. Let's say we want to find all posts that user ola authored. We will use `filter` instead of `all` in `Post.objects.all()`. In parentheses we state what condition(s) a blog post needs to meet to end up in our queryset. In our case, the condition is that `author` should be equal to `me`. The way to write it in Django is `author=me`. Now our piece of code looks like this:

command-line

```
>>> Post.objects.filter(author=me)
[<Post: Sample title>, <Post: Post number  >, <Post: My  rd post!>, <Post:  th title of post>]
```

Or maybe we want to see all the posts that contain the word 'title' in the `title` field?

command-line

```
>>> Post.objects.filter(title__contains='title')
[<Post: Sample title>, <Post:  th title of post>]
```

> There are two underscore characters (_) between `title` and `contains`. Django's ORM uses this rule to separate field names ("title") and operations or filters ("contains"). If you use only one underscore, you'll get an error like "FieldError: Cannot resolve keyword title_contains".

You can also get a list of all published posts. We do this by filtering all the posts that have `published_date` set in the past:

command-line

```
>>> from django.utils import timezone
>>> Post.objects.filter(published_date__lte=timezone.now())
[]
```

Unfortunately, the post we added from the Python console is not published yet. But we can change that! First get an instance of a post we want to publish:

command-line

```
>>> post = Post.objects.get(title="Sample title")
```

And then publish it with our `publish` method:

command-line

```
>>> post.publish()
```

Now try to get list of published posts again (press the up arrow key three times and hit `enter`):

command-line

```
>>> Post.objects.filter(published_date__lte=timezone.now())
[<Post: Sample title>]
```

Ordering objects

QuerySets also allow you to order the list of objects. Let's try to order them by `created_date` field:

command-line

```
>>> Post.objects.order_by('created_date')
[<Post: Sample title>, <Post: Post number  >, <Post: My  rd post!>, <Post:  th title of post>]
```

We can also reverse the ordering by adding - at the beginning:

command-line

```
>>> Post.objects.order_by('-created_date')
[<Post: 4th title of post>, <Post: My 3rd post!>, <Post: Post number 2>, <Post: Sample title>]
```

Chaining QuerySets

You can also combine QuerySets by **chaining** them together:

```
>>> Post.objects.filter(published_date__lte=timezone.now()).order_by('published_date')
```

This is really powerful and lets you write quite complex queries.

Cool! You're now ready for the next part! To close the shell, type this:

command-line

```
>>> exit()
$
```

Dynamic data in templates

We have different pieces in place: the `Post` model is defined in `models.py`, we have `post_list` in `views.py` and the template added. But how will we actually make our posts appear in our HTML template? Because that is what we want to do – take some content (models saved in the database) and display it nicely in our template, right?

This is exactly what *views* are supposed to do: connect models and templates. In our `post_list` *view* we will need to take the models we want to display and pass them to the template. In a *view* we decide what (model) will be displayed in a template.

OK, so how will we achieve this?

We need to open our `blog/views.py`. So far `post_list` *view* looks like this:

blog/views.py

```
from django.shortcuts import render

def post_list(request):
    return render(request, 'blog/post_list.html', {})
```

Remember when we talked about including code written in different files? Now is the moment when we have to include the model we have written in `models.py`. We will add the line `from .models import Post` like this:

blog/views.py

```
from django.shortcuts import render
from .models import Post
```

The dot before `models` means *current directory* or *current application*. Both `views.py` and `models.py` are in the same directory. This means we can use `.` and the name of the file (without `.py`). Then we import the name of the model (`Post`).

But what's next? To take actual blog posts from the `Post` model we need something called `QuerySet`.

QuerySet

You should already be familiar with how QuerySets work. We talked about them in Django ORM (QuerySets) chapter.

So now we want published blog posts sorted by `published_date`, right? We already did that in QuerySets chapter!

blog/views.py

```
Post.objects.filter(published_date__lte=timezone.now()).order_by('published_date')
```

Now we put this piece of code inside the `blog/views.py` file by adding it to the function `def post_list(request)`, but don't forget to first add `from django.utils import timezone` :

blog/views.py

```
from django.shortcuts import render
from django.utils import timezone
from .models import Post

def post_list(request):
    posts = Post.objects.filter(published_date__lte=timezone.now()).order_by('published_date')
    return render(request, 'blog/post_list.html', {})
```

The last missing part is passing the `posts` QuerySet to the template context. Don't worry – we will cover how to display it In a later chapter.

Please note that we create a *variable* for our QuerySet: `posts` . Treat this as the name of our QuerySet. From now on we can refer to it by this name.

In the `render` function we have one parameter `request` (everything we receive from the user via the Internet) and another giving the template file (`'blog/post_list.html'`). The last parameter, `{}` , is a place in which we can add some things for the template to use. We need to give them names (we will stick to `'posts'` right now). :) It should look like this: `{'posts':` `posts}` . Please note that the part before `:` is a string; you need to wrap it with quotes: `''` .

So finally our `blog/views.py` file should look like this:

blog/views.py

```python
from django.shortcuts import render
from django.utils import timezone
from .models import Post

def post_list(request):
    posts = Post.objects.filter(published_date__lte=timezone.now()).order_by('published_date')
    return render(request, 'blog/post_list.html', {'posts': posts})
```

That's it! Time to go back to our template and display this QuerySet!

Want to read a little bit more about QuerySets in Django? You should look here:

https://docs.djangoproject.com/en/1.9/ref/models/querysets/

Django templates

Time to display some data! Django gives us some helpful built-in **template tags** for that.

What are template tags?

You see, in HTML, you can't really write Python code, because browsers don't understand it. They know only HTML. We know that HTML is rather static, while Python is much more dynamic.

Django template tags allow us to transfer Python-like things into HTML, so you can build dynamic websites faster and easier. Cool!

Display post list template

In the previous chapter we gave our template a list of posts in the `posts` variable. Now we will display it in HTML.

To print a variable in Django templates, we use double curly brackets with the variable's name inside, like this:

blog/templates/blog/post_list.html

```
{{ posts }}
```

Try this in your `blog/templates/blog/post_list.html` template. Replace everything from the second `<div>` to the third `</div>` with `{{ posts }}`. Save the file, and refresh the page to see the results:

As you can see, all we've got is this:

blog/templates/blog/post_list.html

```
[<Post: My second post>, <Post: My first post>]
```

This means that Django understands it as a list of objects. Remember from **Introduction to Python** how we can display lists? Yes, with for loops! In a Django template you do them like this:

blog/templates/blog/post_list.html

```
{% for post in posts %}
    {{ post }}
{% endfor %}
```

Try this in your template.

It works! But we want the posts to be displayed like the static posts we created earlier in the **Introduction to HTML** chapter. You can mix HTML and template tags. Our `body` will look like this:

blog/templates/blog/post_list.html

```
<div>
    <h1><a href="/">Django Girls Blog</a></h1>
</div>

{% for post in posts %}
    <div>
        <p>published: {{ post.published_date }}</p>
        <h1><a href="">{{ post.title }}</a></h1>
        <p>{{ post.text|linebreaksbr }}</p>
    </div>
{% endfor %}
```

Everything you put between `{% for %}` and `{% endfor %}` will be repeated for each object in the list. Refresh your page:

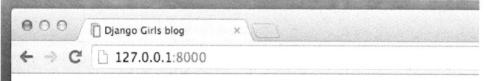

Have you noticed that we used a slightly different notation this time (`{{ post.title }}` or `{{ post.text }}`) ? We are accessing data in each of the fields defined in our `Post` model. Also, the `|linebreaksbr` is piping the posts' text through a filter to convert line-breaks into paragraphs.

One more thing

It'd be good to see if your website will still be working on the public Internet, right? Let's try deploying to PythonAnywhere again. Here's a recap of the steps…

- First, push your code to Github

command-line

```
$ git status
[...]
$ git add --all .
$ git status
[...]
$ git commit -m "Modified templates to display posts from database."
[...]
$ git push
```

- Then, log back in to PythonAnywhere and go to your **Bash console** (or start a new one), and run:

command-line

```
$ cd my-first-blog
$ git pull
[...]
```

- Finally, hop on over to the Web tab and hit **Reload** on your web app. Your update should be live! If the blog posts on your PythonAnywhere site don't match the posts appearing on the blog hosted on your local server, that's OK. The databases on your local computer and Python Anywhere don't sync with the rest of your files.

Congrats! Now go ahead and try adding a new post in your Django admin (remember to add published_date!) Make sure you are in the Django admin for your pythonanywhere site, https://yourname.pythonanywhere.com/admin. Then refresh your page to see if the post appears there.

Works like a charm? We're proud! Step away from your computer for a bit – you have earned a break. :)

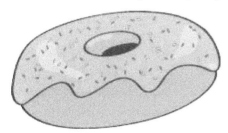

CSS – make it pretty!

Our blog still looks pretty ugly, right? Time to make it nice! We will use CSS for that.

What is CSS?

Cascading Style Sheets (CSS) is a language used for describing the look and formatting of a website written in a markup language (like HTML). Treat it as make-up for our web page. ;)

But we don't want to start from scratch again, right? Once more, we'll use something that programmers released on the Internet for free. Reinventing the wheel is no fun, you know.

Let's use Bootstrap!

Bootstrap is one of the most popular HTML and CSS frameworks for developing beautiful websites: https://getbootstrap.com/

It was written by programmers who worked for Twitter. Now it's developed by volunteers from all over the world!

Install Bootstrap

To install Bootstrap, you need to add this to your `<head>` in your `.html` file:

blog/templates/blog/post_list.html

```
<link rel="stylesheet" href="//maxcdn.bootstrapcdn.com/bootstrap/3.2.0/css/bootstrap.min.css">
<link rel="stylesheet" href="//maxcdn.bootstrapcdn.com/bootstrap/3.2.0/css/bootstrap-theme.min.css">
```

This doesn't add any files to your project. It just points to files that exist on the Internet. Just go ahead, open your website and refresh the page. Here it is!

Looking nicer already!

Static files in Django

Finally we will take a closer look at these things we've been calling **static files**. Static files are all your CSS and images. Their content doesn't depend on the request context and will be the same for every user.

Where to put static files for Django

Django already knows where to find the static files for the built-in "admin" app. Now we just need to add some static files for our own app, `blog`.

We do that by creating a folder called `static` inside the blog app:

```
djangogirls
├── blog
|   ├── migrations
|   └── static
└── mysite
```

Django will automatically find any folders called "static" inside any of your apps' folders. Then it will be able to use their contents as static files.

Your first CSS file!

Let's create a CSS file now, to add your own style to your web page. Create a new directory called `css` inside your `static` directory. Then create a new file called `blog.css` inside this `css` directory. Ready?

```
djangogirls
└── blog
        └── static
                └── css
                        └── blog.css
```

Time to write some CSS! Open up the `blog/static/css/blog.css` file in your code editor.

We won't be going too deep into customizing and learning about CSS here. It's pretty easy and you can learn it on your own after this workshop. There is a recommendation for a free course to learn more at the end of this page.

But let's do at least a little. Maybe we could change the color of our header? To understand colors, computers use special codes. These codes start with `#` followed by 6 letters (A–F) and numbers (0–9). For example, the code for blue is `#0000FF`. You can find the color codes for many colors here: http://www.colorpicker.com/. You may also use predefined colors, such as `red` and `green`.

In your `blog/static/css/blog.css` file you should add the following code:

blog/static/css/blog.css

```
h1 a {
    color: #FCA205;
}
```

`h1 a` is a CSS Selector. This means we're applying our styles to any `a` element inside of an `h1` element. So when we have something like `<h1><a href="">link</a></h1>`, the `h1 a` style will apply. In this case, we're telling it to change its color to `#FCA205`, which is orange. Of course, you can put your own color here!

In a CSS file we determine styles for elements in the HTML file. The first way we identify elements is with the element name. You might remember these as tags from the HTML section. Things like `a`, `h1`, and `body` are all examples of element names. We also identify elements by the attribute `class` or the attribute `id`. Class and id are names you give the element by yourself. Classes define groups of elements, and ids point to specific elements. For example, you could identify the following tag by using the tag name `a`, the class `external_link`, or the id `link_to_wiki_page`:

```
<a href="https://en.wikipedia.org/wiki/Django" class="external_link" id="link_to_wiki_page">
```

You can read more about CSS Selectors at w3schools.

We also need to tell our HTML template that we added some CSS. Open the `blog/templates/blog/post_list.html` file and add this line at the very beginning of it:

blog/templates/blog/post_list.html

```
{% load staticfiles %}
```

We're just loading static files here. :) Between the `<head>` and `</head>` tags, after the links to the Bootstrap CSS files, add this line:

blog/templates/blog/post_list.html

```
<link rel="stylesheet" href="{% static 'css/blog.css' %}">
```

The browser reads the files in the order they're given, so we need to make sure this is in the right place. Otherwise the code in our file may override code in Bootstrap files. We just told our template where our CSS file is located.

Your file should now look like this:

blog/templates/blog/post_list.html

```
{% load staticfiles %}
<html>
    <head>
        <title>Django Girls blog</title>
        <link rel="stylesheet" href="//maxcdn.bootstrapcdn.com/bootstrap/3.2.0/css/bootstrap.min.css">
        <link rel="stylesheet" href="//maxcdn.bootstrapcdn.com/bootstrap/3.2.0/css/bootstrap-theme.min.css">
        <link rel="stylesheet" href="{% static 'css/blog.css' %}">
    </head>
    <body>
        <div>
            <h1><a href="/">Django Girls Blog</a></h1>
        </div>

        {% for post in posts %}
            <div>
                <p>published: {{ post.published_date }}</p>
                <h1><a href="">{{ post.title }}</a></h1>
                <p>{{ post.text|linebreaksbr }}</p>
            </div>
        {% endfor %}
    </body>
</html>
```

OK, save the file and refresh the site!

Nice work! Maybe we would also like to give our website a little air and increase the margin on the left side? Let's try this!

blog/static/css/blog.css

```css
body {
    padding-left: 15px;
}
```

Add that to your CSS, save the file and see how it works!

Maybe we can customize the font in our header? Paste this into your `<head>` in `blog/templates/blog/post_list.html` file:

blog/templates/blog/post_list.html

```html
<link href="//fonts.googleapis.com/css?family=Lobster&subset=latin,latin-ext" rel="stylesheet" type="text/css">
```

As before, check the order and place before the link to `blog/static/css/blog.css`. This line will import a font called *Lobster* from Google Fonts (https://www.google.com/fonts).

Find the `h1 a` declaration block (the code between braces `{` and `}`) in the CSS file `blog/static/css/blog.css`. Now add the line `font-family: 'Lobster';` between the braces, and refresh the page:

blog/static/css/blog.css

```
h1 a {
    color: #FCA205;
    font-family: 'Lobster';
}
```

Great!

As mentioned above, CSS has a concept of classes. These allow you to name a part of the HTML code and apply styles only to this part, without affecting other parts. This can be super helpful! Maybe you have two divs that are doing something different (like your header and your post). A class can help you make them look different.

Go ahead and name some parts of the HTML code. Add a class called `page-header` to your `div` that contains your header, like this:

blog/templates/blog/post_list.html

```
<div class="page-header">
    <h1><a href="/">Django Girls Blog</a></h1>
</div>
```

And now add a class `post` to your `div` containing a blog post.

blog/templates/blog/post_list.html

```
<div class="post">
    <p>published: {{ post.published_date }}</p>
    <h1><a href="">{{ post.title }}</a></h1>
    <p>{{ post.text|linebreaksbr }}</p>
</div>
```

We will now add declaration blocks to different selectors. Selectors starting with `.` relate to classes. There are many great tutorials and explanations about CSS on the Web that can help you understand the following code. For now, just copy and paste it into your `blog/static/css/blog.css` file:

blog/static/css/blog.css

```css
.page-header {
    background-color: #ff2400;
    margin-top: 0;
    padding: 20px 20px 20px 40px;
}

.page-header h1, .page-header h1 a, .page-header h1 a:visited, .page-header h1 a:active {
    color: #ffffff;
    font-size: 36pt;
    text-decoration: none;
}

.content {
    margin-left: 40px;
}

h1, h2, h3, h4 {
    font-family: 'Lobster', cursive;
}

.date {
    color: #828282;
}

.save {
    float: right;
}

.post-form textarea, .post-form input {
    width: 100%;
}

.top-menu, .top-menu:hover, .top-menu:visited {
    color: #ffffff;
    float: right;
    font-size: 26pt;
    margin-right: 20px;
}

.post {
    margin-bottom: 70px;
}

.post h1 a, .post h1 a:visited {
    color: #000000;
}
```

Then surround the HTML code which displays the posts with declarations of classes. Replace this:

blog/templates/blog/post_list.html

```
{% for post in posts %}
    <div class="post">
        <p>published: {{ post.published_date }}</p>
        <h1><a href="">{{ post.title }}</a></h1>
        <p>{{ post.text|linebreaksbr }}</p>
    </div>
{% endfor %}
```

in the blog/templates/blog/post_list.html with this:

blog/templates/blog/post_list.html

```
<div class="content container">
    <div class="row">
        <div class="col-md-8">
            {% for post in posts %}
                <div class="post">
                    <div class="date">
                        <p>published: {{ post.published_date }}</p>
                    </div>
                    <h1><a href="">{{ post.title }}</a></h1>
                    <p>{{ post.text|linebreaksbr }}</p>
                </div>
            {% endfor %}
        </div>
    </div>
</div>
```

Save those files and refresh your website.

Woohoo! Looks awesome, right? Look at the code we just pasted to find the places where we added classes in the HTML and used them in the CSS. Where would you make the change if you wanted the date to be turquoise?

Don't be afraid to tinker with this CSS a little bit and try to change some things. Playing with the CSS can help you understand what the different things are doing. If you break something, don't worry – you can always undo it!

We really recommend taking this free online Codeacademy HTML & CSS course. It can help you learn all about making your websites prettier with CSS.

Ready for the next chapter?! :)

Template extending

Another nice thing Django has for you is **template extending**. What does this mean? It means that you can use the same parts of your HTML for different pages of your website.

Templates help when you want to use the same information or layout in more than one place. You don't have to repeat yourself in every file. And if you want to change something, you don't have to do it in every template, just one!

Create a base template

A base template is the most basic template that you extend on every page of your website.

Let's create a `base.html` file in `blog/templates/blog/` :

```
blog
└──templates
    └──blog
            base.html
            post_list.html
```

Then open it up and copy everything from `post_list.html` to `base.html` file, like this:

blog/templates/blog/base.html

```
{% load staticfiles %}
<html>
    <head>
        <title>Django Girls blog</title>
        <link rel="stylesheet" href="//maxcdn.bootstrapcdn.com/bootstrap/3.2.0/css/bootstrap.min.css">
        <link rel="stylesheet" href="//maxcdn.bootstrapcdn.com/bootstrap/3.2.0/css/bootstrap-theme.min.css">
        <link href='//fonts.googleapis.com/css?family=Lobster&subset=latin,latin-ext' rel='stylesheet' type='text/css'>
        <link rel="stylesheet" href="{% static 'css/blog.css' %}">
    </head>
    <body>
        <div class="page-header">
            <h1><a href="/">Django Girls Blog</a></h1>
        </div>

        <div class="content container">
            <div class="row">
                <div class="col-md-8">
                {% for post in posts %}
                    <div class="post">
                        <div class="date">
                            {{ post.published_date }}
                        </div>
                        <h1><a href="">{{ post.title }}</a></h1>
                        <p>{{ post.text|linebreaksbr }}</p>
                    </div>
                {% endfor %}
                </div>
            </div>
        </div>
    </body>
</html>
```

Then in `base.html` , replace your whole `<body>` (everything between `<body>` and `</body>`) with this:

blog/templates/blog/base.html

```
<body>
    <div class="page-header">
        <h1><a href="/">Django Girls Blog</a></h1>
    </div>
    <div class="content container">
        <div class="row">
            <div class="col-md-8">
            {% block content %}
            {% endblock %}
            </div>
        </div>
    </div>
</body>
```

You might notice this replaced everything from `{% for post in posts %}` to `{% endfor %}` with:

blog/templates/blog/base.html

```
{% block content %}
{% endblock %}
```

But why? You just created a `block`! You used the template tag `{% block %}` to make an area that will have HTML inserted in it. That HTML will come from another template that extends this template (`base.html`). We will show you how to do this in a moment.

Now save `base.html` and open your `blog/templates/blog/post_list.html` again. You're going to remove everything above `{% for post in posts %}` and below `{% endfor %}` . When you're done, the file will look like this:

blog/templates/blog/post_list.html

```
{% for post in posts %}
    <div class="post">
        <div class="date">
            {{ post.published_date }}
        </div>
        <h1><a href="">{{ post.title }}</a></h1>
        <p>{{ post.text|linebreaksbr }}</p>
    </div>
{% endfor %}
```

We want to use this as part of our template for all the content blocks. Time to add block tags to this file!

You want your block tag to match the tag in your `base.html` file. You also want it to include all the code that belongs in your content blocks. To do that, put everything between `{% block content %}` and `{% endblock content %}` . Like this:

blog/templates/blog/post_list.html

```
{% block content %}
    {% for post in posts %}
        <div class="post">
            <div class="date">
                {{ post.published_date }}
            </div>
            <h1><a href="">{{ post.title }}</a></h1>
            <p>{{ post.text|linebreaksbr }}</p>
        </div>
    {% endfor %}
{% endblock %}
```

Only one thing left. We need to connect these two templates together. This is what extending templates is all about! We'll do this by adding an extends tag to the beginning of the file. Like this:

blog/templates/blog/post_list.html

```
{% extends 'blog/base.html' %}

{% block content %}
    {% for post in posts %}
        <div class="post">
            <div class="date">
                {{ post.published_date }}
            </div>
            <h1><a href="">{{ post.title }}</a></h1>
            <p>{{ post.text|linebreaksbr }}</p>
        </div>
    {% endfor %}
{% endblock %}
```

That's it! Check if your website is still working properly. :)

If you get the error `TemplateDoesNotExist`, that means that there is no `blog/base.html` file and you have `runserver` running in the console. Try to stop it (by pressing Ctrl+C – the Control and C keys together) and restart it by running a `python manage.py runserver` command.

Extend your application

We've already completed all the different steps necessary for the creation of our website: we know how to write a model, url, view and template. We also know how to make our website pretty.

Time to practice!

The first thing we need in our blog is, obviously, a page to display one post, right?

We already have a `Post` model, so we don't need to add anything to `models.py` .

Create a template link to a post's detail

We will start with adding a link inside `blog/templates/blog/post_list.html` file. So far it should look like this:

blog/templates/blog/post_list.html

```
{% extends 'blog/base.html' %}

{% block content %}
    {% for post in posts %}
        <div class="post">
            <div class="date">
                {{ post.published_date }}
            </div>
            <h1><a href="">{{ post.title }}</a></h1>
            <p>{{ post.text|linebreaksbr }}</p>
        </div>
    {% endfor %}
{% endblock content %}
```

We want to have a link from a post's title in the post list to the post's detail page. Let's change `<h1><a href="">{{ post.title }}</a></h1>` so that it links to the post's detail page:

blog/templates/blog/post_list.html

```
<h1><a href="{% url 'post_detail' pk=post.pk %}">{{ post.title }}</a></h1>
```

Time to explain the mysterious `{% url 'post_detail' pk=post.pk %}` . As you might suspect, the `{% %}` notation means that we are using Django template tags. This time we will use one that will create a URL for us!

`blog.views.post_detail` is a path to a `post_detail` *view* we want to create. Please note: `blog` is the name of our application (the directory `blog`), `views` is from the name of the `views.py` file and the last bit – `post_detail` – is the name of the *view*.

And how about `pk=post.pk` ? `pk` is short for primary key, which is a unique name for each record in a database. Because we didn't specify a primary key in our `Post` model, Django creates one for us (by default, a number that increases by one for each record, i.e. 1, 2, 3) and adds it as a field named `pk` to each of our posts. We access the primary key by writing `post.pk` , the same way we access other fields (`title` , `author` , etc.) in our `Post` object!

Now when we go to http://127.0.0.1:8000/ we will have an error (as expected, since we don't have a URL or a *view* for `post_detail`). It will look like this:

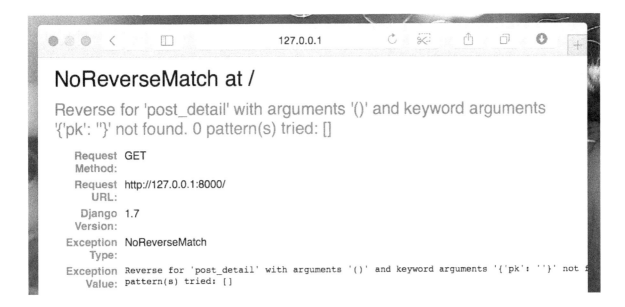

Create a URL to a post's detail

Let's create a URL in `urls.py` for our `post_detail` *view*!

We want our first post's detail to be displayed at this **URL**: http://127.0.0.1:8000/post/1/

Let's make a URL in the `blog/urls.py` file to point Django to a *view* named `post_detail`, that will show an entire blog post. Add the line `url(r'^post/(?P<pk>\d+)/$', views.post_detail, name='post_detail'),` to the `blog/urls.py` file. The file should look like this:

blog/urls.py

```
from django.conf.urls import url
from . import views

urlpatterns = [
    url(r'^$', views.post_list, name='post_list'),
    url(r'^post/(?P<pk>\d+)/$', views.post_detail, name='post_detail'),
]
```

This part `^post/(?P<pk>\d+)/$` looks scary, but no worries – we will explain it for you:

- it starts with `^` again – "the beginning".
- `post/` just means that after the beginning, the URL should contain the word **post** and a /. So far so good.
- `(?P<pk>\d+)` – this part is trickier. It means that Django will take everything that you place here and transfer it to a view as a variable called `pk`. (Note that this matches the name we gave the primary key variable back in `blog/templates/blog/post_list.html` !) `\d` also tells us that it can only be a digit, not a letter (so everything between 0 and 9). `+` means that there needs to be one or more digits there. So something like `http://127.0.0.1:8000/post//` is not valid, but `http://127.0.0.1:8000/post/1234567890/` is perfectly OK!
- `/` – then we need a / again.
- `$` – "the end"!

That means if you enter `http://127.0.0.1:8000/post/5/` into your browser, Django will understand that you are looking for a *view* called `post_detail` and transfer the information that `pk` equals `5` to that *view*.

OK, we've added a new URL pattern to `blog/urls.py` ! Let's refresh the page: http://127.0.0.1:8000/ Boom! The server has stopped running again. Have a look at the console – as expected, there's yet another error!

```
    return _bootstrap._gcd_import(name[level:], package, level)
  File "<frozen importlib._bootstrap>", line 2231, in _gcd_import
  File "<frozen importlib._bootstrap>", line 2214, in _find_and_load
  File "<frozen importlib._bootstrap>", line 2203, in _find_and_load_unlocked
  File "<frozen importlib._bootstrap>", line 1200, in _load_unlocked
  File "<frozen importlib._bootstrap>", line 1129, in _exec
  File "<frozen importlib._bootstrap>", line 1448, in exec_module
  File "<frozen importlib._bootstrap>", line 321, in _call_with_frames_removed
  File "/home/hel/code/djangogirls/workthrough/blog/urls.py", line 6, in <module>
    url(r'^post/(?P<pk>[0-9]+)/$', views.post_detail, name='post_detail'),
AttributeError: 'module' object has no attribute 'post_detail'
```

Do you remember what the next step is? Of course: adding a view!

Add a post's detail view

This time our *view* is given an extra parameter, `pk` . Our *view* needs to catch it, right? So we will define our function as `def post_detail(request, pk):` . Note that we need to use exactly the same name as the one we specified in urls (`pk`). Omitting this variable is incorrect and will result in an error!

Now, we want to get one and only one blog post. To do this, we can use querysets, like this:

blog/views.py

```
Post.objects.get(pk=pk)
```

But this code has a problem. If there is no `Post` with the given `primary key` (`pk`) we will have a super ugly error!

We don't want that! But, of course, Django comes with something that will handle that for us: `get_object_or_404` . In case there is no `Post` with the given `pk` , it will display much nicer page, the `Page Not Found 404` page.

Page not found (404)

Request Method: GET
Request URL: http://127.0.0.1:8000/post/10/

No Post matches the given query.

The good news is that you can actually create your own `Page not found` page and make it as pretty as you want. But it's not super important right now, so we will skip it.

OK, time to add a *view* to our `views.py` file!

We should open `blog/views.py` and add the following code near the other `from` lines:

blog/views.py

```
from django.shortcuts import render, get_object_or_404
```

And at the end of the file we will add our *view*:

blog/views.py

```
def post_detail(request, pk):
    post = get_object_or_404(Post, pk=pk)
    return render(request, 'blog/post_detail.html', {'post': post})
```

Yes. It is time to refresh the page: http://127.0.0.1:8000/

It worked! But what happens when you click a link in blog post title?

Oh no! Another error! But we already know how to deal with it, right? We need to add a template!

Create a template for the post details

We will create a file in `blog/templates/blog` called `post_detail.html`.

It will look like this:

blog/templates/blog/post_detail.html

```
{% extends 'blog/base.html' %}

{% block content %}
    <div class="post">
        {% if post.published_date %}
            <div class="date">
                {{ post.published_date }}
            </div>
        {% endif %}
        <h1>{{ post.title }}</h1>
        <p>{{ post.text|linebreaksbr }}</p>
    </div>
{% endblock %}
```

Once again we are extending `base.html` . In the `content` block we want to display a post's published_date (if it exists), title and text. But we should discuss some important things, right?

`{% if ... %}` ... `{% endif %}` is a template tag we can use when we want to check something. (Remember `if ... else .. ` from **Introduction to Python** chapter?) In this scenario we want to check if a post's `published_date` is not empty.

OK, we can refresh our page and see if `TemplateDoesNotExist` is gone now.

Yay! It works!

One more thing: deploy time!

It'd be good to see if your website will still be working on PythonAnywhere, right? Let's try deploying again.

command-line

```
$ git status
$ git add --all .
$ git status
$ git commit -m "Added view and template for detailed blog post as well as CSS for the site."
$ git push
```

Then, in a PythonAnywhere Bash console:

command-line

```
$ cd my-first-blog
$ git pull
[...]
```

Finally, hop on over to the Web tab and hit **Reload**.

And that should be it! Congrats :)

Django Forms

The final thing we want to do on our website is create a nice way to add and edit blog posts. Django's `admin` is cool, but it is rather hard to customize and make pretty. With `forms` we will have absolute power over our interface – we can do almost anything we can imagine!

The nice thing about Django forms is that we can either define one from scratch or create a `ModelForm` which will save the result of the form to the model.

This is exactly what we want to do: we will create a form for our `Post` model.

Like every important part of Django, forms have their own file: `forms.py`.

We need to create a file with this name in the `blog` directory.

```
blog
└── forms.py
```

OK, let's open it and type the following code:

blog/forms.py

```python
from django import forms

from .models import Post

class PostForm(forms.ModelForm):

    class Meta:
        model = Post
        fields = ('title', 'text',)
```

We need to import Django forms first (`from django import forms`) and, obviously, our `Post` model (`from .models import Post`).

`PostForm`, as you probably suspect, is the name of our form. We need to tell Django that this form is a `ModelForm` (so Django will do some magic for us) – `forms.ModelForm` is responsible for that.

Next, we have `class Meta`, where we tell Django which model should be used to create this form (`model = Post`).

Finally, we can say which field(s) should end up in our form. In this scenario we want only `title` and `text` to be exposed – `author` should be the person who is currently logged in (you!) and `created_date` should be automatically set when we create a post (i.e. in the code), right?

And that's it! All we need to do now is use the form in a *view* and display it in a template.

So once again we will create a link to the page, a URL, a view and a template.

Link to a page with the form

It's time to open `blog/templates/blog/base.html`. We will add a link in `div` named `page-header` :

blog/templates/blog/base.html

```html
<a href="{% url 'post_new' %}" class="top-menu"><span class="glyphicon glyphicon-plus"></span></a>
```

Note that we want to call our new view `post_new`. The class `"glyphicon glyphicon-plus"` is provided by the bootstrap theme we are using, and will display a plus sign for us.

After adding the line, your HTML file should now look like this:

blog/templates/blog/base.html

```
{% load staticfiles %}
<html>
    <head>
        <title>Django Girls blog</title>
        <link rel="stylesheet" href="//maxcdn.bootstrapcdn.com/bootstrap/3.2.0/css/bootstrap.min.css">
        <link rel="stylesheet" href="//maxcdn.bootstrapcdn.com/bootstrap/3.2.0/css/bootstrap-theme.min.css">
        <link href='//fonts.googleapis.com/css?family=Lobster&subset=latin,latin-ext' rel='stylesheet' type='text/css'
>
        <link rel="stylesheet" href="{% static 'css/blog.css' %}">
    </head>
    <body>
        <div class="page-header">
            <a href="{% url 'post_new' %}" class="top-menu"><span class="glyphicon glyphicon-plus"></span></a>
            <h1><a href="/">Django Girls Blog</a></h1>
        </div>
        <div class="content container">
            <div class="row">
                <div class="col-md-8">
                    {% block content %}
                    {% endblock %}
                </div>
            </div>
        </div>
    </body>
</html>
```

After saving and refreshing the page http://127.0.0.1:8000 you will obviously see a familiar NoReverseMatch error, right?

URL

We open blog/urls.py and add a line:

blog/urls.py

```
url(r'^post/new/$', views.post_new, name='post_new'),
```

And the final code will look like this:

blog/urls.py

```
from django.conf.urls import url
from . import views

urlpatterns = [
    url(r'^$', views.post_list, name='post_list'),
    url(r'^post/(?P<pk>\d+)/$', views.post_detail, name='post_detail'),
    url(r'^post/new/$', views.post_new, name='post_new'),
]
```

After refreshing the site, we see an AttributeError, since we don't have the post_new view implemented. Let's add it right now.

post_new view

Time to open the blog/views.py file and add the following lines with the rest of the from rows:

blog/views.py

```
from .forms import PostForm
```

And then our *view*:

blog/views.py

```
def post_new(request):
    form = PostForm()
    return render(request, 'blog/post_edit.html', {'form': form})
```

To create a new `Post` form, we need to call `PostForm()` and pass it to the template. We will go back to this *view*, but for now, let's quickly create a template for the form.

Template

We need to create a file `post_edit.html` in the `blog/templates/blog` directory. To make a form work we need several things:

- We have to display the form. We can do that with (for example) a simple `{{ form.as_p }}`.
- The line above needs to be wrapped with an HTML form tag: `<form method="POST">...</form>`.
- We need a `save` button. We do that with an HTML button: `<button type="submit">Save</button>`.
- And finally, just after the opening `<form ...>` tag we need to add `{% csrf_token %}`. This is very important, since it makes your forms secure! If you forget about this bit, Django will complain when you try to save the form:

OK, so let's see how the HTML in `post_edit.html` should look:

blog/templates/blog/post_edit.html

```
{% extends 'blog/base.html' %}

{% block content %}
    <h1>New post</h1>
    <form method="POST" class="post-form">{% csrf_token %}
        {{ form.as_p }}
        <button type="submit" class="save btn btn-default">Save</button>
    </form>
{% endblock %}
```

Time to refresh! Yay! Your form is displayed!

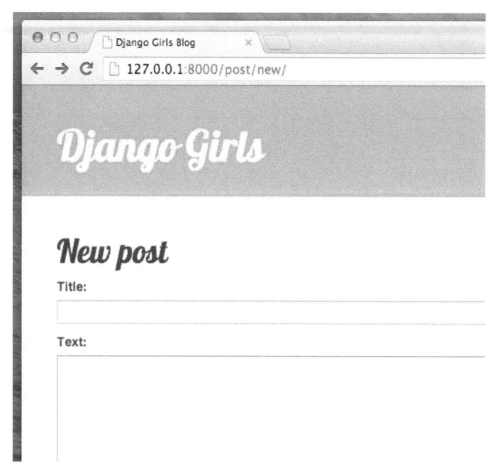

But, wait a minute! When you type something in the `title` and `text` fields and try to save it, what will happen?

Nothing! We are once again on the same page and our text is gone… and no new post is added. So what went wrong?

The answer is: nothing. We need to do a little bit more work in our *view*.

Saving the form

Open `blog/views.py` once again. Currently all we have in the `post_new` view is the following:

blog/views.py

```
def post_new(request):
    form = PostForm()
    return render(request, 'blog/post_edit.html', {'form': form})
```

When we submit the form, we are brought back to the same view, but this time we have some more data in `request`, more specifically in `request.POST` (the naming has nothing to do with a blog "post"; it's to do with the fact that we're "posting" data). Remember how in the HTML file, our `<form>` definition had the variable `method="POST"` ? All the fields from the form are now in `request.POST`. You should not rename `POST` to anything else (the only other valid value for `method` is `GET`, but we have no time to explain what the difference is).

So in our *view* we have two separate situations to handle: first, when we access the page for the first time and we want a blank form, and second, when we go back to the *view* with all form data we just typed. So we need to add a condition (we will use `if` for that):

blog/views.py

```
if request.method == "POST":
    [...]
else:
    form = PostForm()
```

It's time to fill in the dots `[...]` . If `method` is POST then we want to construct the `PostForm` with data from the form, right? We will do that as follows:

blog/views.py

```
form = PostForm(request.POST)
```

Easy! The next thing is to check if the form is correct (all required fields are set and no incorrect values have been submitted). We do that with `form.is_valid()` .

We check if the form is valid and if so, we can save it!

blog/views.py

```
if form.is_valid():
    post = form.save(commit=False)
    post.author = request.user
    post.published_date = timezone.now()
    post.save()
```

Basically, we have two things here: we save the form with `form.save` and we add an author (since there was no `author` field in the `PostForm` and this field is required). `commit=False` means that we don't want to save the `Post` model yet – we want to add the author first. Most of the time you will use `form.save()` without `commit=False` , but in this case, we need to supply it. `post.save()` will preserve changes (adding the author) and a new blog post is created!

Finally, it would be awesome if we could immediately go to the `post_detail` page for our newly created blog post, right? To do that we need one more import:

blog/views.py

```
from django.shortcuts import redirect
```

Add it at the very beginning of your file. And now we can say, "go to the `post_detail` page for the newly created post":

blog/views.py

```
return redirect('post_detail', pk=post.pk)
```

`post_detail` is the name of the view we want to go to. Remember that this *view* requires a `pk` variable? To pass it to the views, we use `pk=post.pk` , where `post` is the newly created blog post!

OK, we've talked a lot, but we probably want to see what the whole *view* looks like now, right?

blog/views.py

```
def post_new(request):
    if request.method == "POST":
        form = PostForm(request.POST)
        if form.is_valid():
            post = form.save(commit=False)
            post.author = request.user
            post.published_date = timezone.now()
            post.save()
            return redirect('post_detail', pk=post.pk)
    else:
        form = PostForm()
    return render(request, 'blog/post_edit.html', {'form': form})
```

Let's see if it works. Go to the page http://127.0.0.1:8000/post/new/, add a `title` and `text`, save it... and voilà! The new blog post is added and we are redirected to the `post_detail` page!

You might have noticed that we are setting the publish date before saving the post. Later on, we will introduce a *publish button* in **Django Girls Tutorial: Extensions**.

That is awesome!

> As we have recently used the Django admin interface, the system currently thinks we are still logged in. There are a few situations that could lead to us being logged out (closing the browser, restarting the DB, etc.). If, when creating a post, you find that you are getting errors referring to the lack of a logged-in user, head to the admin page http://127.0.0.1:8000/admin and log in again. This will fix the issue temporarily. There is a permanent fix awaiting you in the **Homework: add security to your website!** chapter after the main tutorial.

localhost:8000/post/new/

ValueError at /post/new/

Cannot assign "<SimpleLazyObject: <django.contrib.auth.models.AnonymousUser object at 0x3264b50>>": "Post.author" must be a "User" instance.

```
Request Method:  POST
   Request URL:  http://localhost:8000/post/new/
Django Version:  1.6.5
Exception Type:  ValueError
Exception Value: Cannot assign "<SimpleLazyObject: <django.contrib.auth.models.AnonymousUser object at 0x3264b50>>": "Post.author" must be a "User" instance.
```

Form validation

Now, we will show you how cool Django forms are. A blog post needs to have `title` and `text` fields. In our `Post` model we did not say that these fields (as opposed to `published_date`) are not required, so Django, by default, expects them to be set.

Try to save the form without `title` and `text`. Guess what will happen!

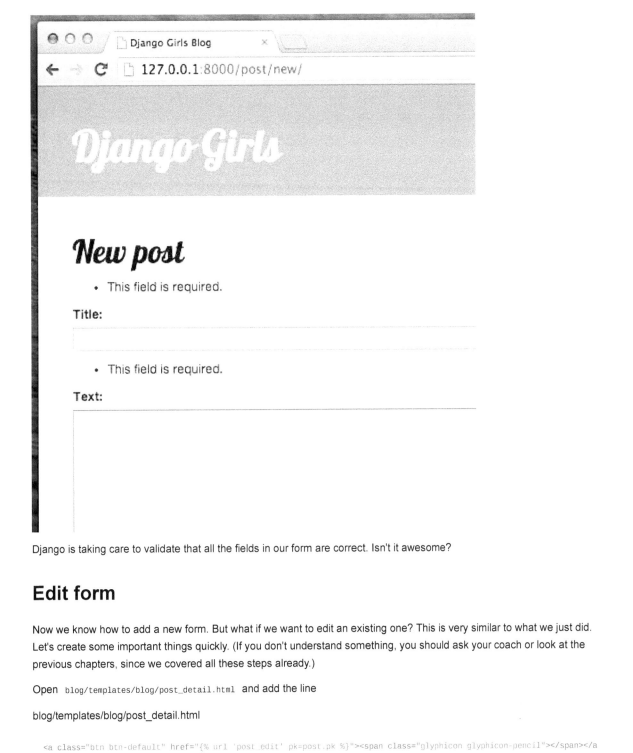

Django is taking care to validate that all the fields in our form are correct. Isn't it awesome?

Edit form

Now we know how to add a new form. But what if we want to edit an existing one? This is very similar to what we just did. Let's create some important things quickly. (If you don't understand something, you should ask your coach or look at the previous chapters, since we covered all these steps already.)

Open `blog/templates/blog/post_detail.html` and add the line

blog/templates/blog/post_detail.html

```
<a class="btn btn-default" href="{% url 'post_edit' pk=post.pk %}"><span class="glyphicon glyphicon-pencil"></span></a
>
```

so that the template will look like this:

blog/templates/blog/post_detail.html

```
{% extends 'blog/base.html' %}

{% block content %}
    <div class="post">
        {% if post.published_date %}
            <div class="date">
                {{ post.published_date }}
            </div>
        {% endif %}
        <a class="btn btn-default" href="{% url 'post_edit' pk=post.pk %}"><span class="glyphicon glyphicon-pencil"></
span></a>
        <h1>{{ post.title }}</h1>
        <p>{{ post.text|linebreaksbr }}</p>
    </div>
{% endblock %}
```

In `blog/urls.py` we add this line:

blog/urls.py

```
url(r'^post/(?P<pk>\d+)/edit/$', views.post_edit, name='post_edit'),
```

We will reuse the template `blog/templates/blog/post_edit.html` , so the last missing thing is a *view*.

Let's open `blog/views.py` and add this at the very end of the file:

blog/views.py

```
def post_edit(request, pk):
    post = get_object_or_404(Post, pk=pk)
    if request.method == "POST":
        form = PostForm(request.POST, instance=post)
        if form.is_valid():
            post = form.save(commit=False)
            post.author = request.user
            post.published_date = timezone.now()
            post.save()
            return redirect('post_detail', pk=post.pk)
    else:
        form = PostForm(instance=post)
    return render(request, 'blog/post_edit.html', {'form': form})
```

This looks almost exactly the same as our `post_new` view, right? But not entirely. For one, we pass an extra `pk` parameter from urls. Next, we get the `Post` model we want to edit with `get_object_or_404(Post, pk=pk)` and then, when we create a form, we pass this post as an `instance` , both when we save the form…

blog/views.py

```
form = PostForm(request.POST, instance=post)
```

…and when we've just opened a form with this post to edit:

blog/views.py

```
form = PostForm(instance=post)
```

OK, let's test if it works! Let's go to the `post_detail` page. There should be an edit button in the top-right corner:

When you click it you will see the form with our blog post:

Feel free to change the title or the text and save the changes!

Congratulations! Your application is getting more and more complete!

If you need more information about Django forms, you should read the documentation:

https://docs.djangoproject.com/en/1.10/topics/forms/

Security

Being able to create new posts just by clicking a link is awesome! But right now, anyone who visits your site will be able to make a new blog post, and that's probably not something you want. Let's make it so the button shows up for you but not for anyone else.

In `blog/templates/blog/base.html`, find our `page-header` `div` and the anchor tag you put in there earlier. It should look like this:

blog/templates/blog/base.html

```
<a href="{% url 'post_new' %}" class="top-menu"><span class="glyphicon glyphicon-plus"></span></a>
```

We're going to add another `{% if %}` tag to this, which will make the link show up only for users who are logged into the admin. Right now, that's just you! Change the `<a>` tag to look like this:

blog/templates/blog/base.html

```
{% if user.is_authenticated %}
    <a href="{% url 'post_new' %}" class="top-menu"><span class="glyphicon glyphicon-plus"></span></a>
{% endif %}
```

This `{% if %}` will cause the link to be sent to the browser only if the user requesting the page is logged in. This doesn't protect the creation of new posts completely, but it's a good first step. We'll cover more security in the extension lessons.

Remember the edit icon we just added to our detail page? We also want to add the same change there, so other people won't be able to edit existing posts.

Open `blog/templates/blog/post_detail.html` and find this line:

blog/templates/blog/post_detail.html

```
<a class="btn btn-default" href="{% url 'post_edit' pk=post.pk %}"><span class="glyphicon glyphicon-pencil"></span></a
>
```

Change it to this:

blog/templates/blog/post_detail.html

```
{% if user.is_authenticated %}
    <a class="btn btn-default" href="{% url 'post_edit' pk=post.pk %}"><span class="glyphicon glyphicon-pencil"></sp
an></a>
{% endif %}
```

Since you're likely logged in, if you refresh the page, you won't see anything different. Load the page in a different browser or an incognito window, though, and you'll see that the link doesn't show up, and the icon doesn't display either!

One more thing: deploy time!

Let's see if all this works on PythonAnywhere. Time for another deploy!

- First, commit your new code, and push it up to Github:

command-line

```
$ git status
$ git add --all .
$ git status
$ git commit -m "Added views to create/edit blog post inside the site."
$ git push
```

- **Then, in a** PythonAnywhere Bash console:

command-line

```
$ cd my-first-blog
$ git pull
[...]
```

- Finally, hop on over to the Web tab and hit **Reload**.

And that should be it! Congrats :)

What's next?

Congratulate yourself! **You're totally awesome**. We're proud! <3

What to do now?

Take a break and relax. You have just done something really huge.

After that, make sure to follow Django Girls on Facebook or Twitter to stay up to date.

Can you recommend any further resources?

Yes! First, go ahead and try our other book, called Django Girls Tutorial: Extensions.

Later on, you can try the resources listed below. They're all very recommended!

- Django's official tutorial
- New Coder tutorials
- Code Academy Python course
- Code Academy HTML & CSS course
- Django Carrots tutorial
- Learn Python The Hard Way book
- Getting Started With Django video lessons
- Two Scoops of Django: Best Practices for Django 1.8 book
- Hello Web App: Learn How to Build a Web App

www.ingramcontent.com/pod-product-compliance
Lightning Source LLC
LaVergne TN
LVHW060144070326
832902LV00018B/2942